Praise for Ken Scholen's prior work on reverse mortgages

Rates a 10 . . . an ideal study book for senior citizens.

Los Angeles Times

An easily understood nuts-and-bolts guide to reverse mortgages.

New York Times

The acknowledged national expert of the reverse mortgages movement.

San Francisco Examiner

The definitive guide to reverse mortgages.

Modern Maturity

Easily readable . . . the best and most in-depth treatment of reverse mortgages.

Philadelphia Inquirer

Eye-opening - packed with rare information.

Midwest Book Review

The bible of reverse mortgages.

Guide to Retirement Living

Enormously useful . . . the most detailed and comprehensive guide to reverse mortgages.

Jane Bryant Quinn

The leading authority on reverse mortgages.

Los Angeles Times

Detailed information on how these programs work . . . advantages and disadvantages.

New York Times

Well-organized, well-presented, everything you ever thought you wanted to know about reverse mortgages.

Small Press Magazine

Easy to understand . . . you'll know what you're doing when you finish it.

Scripps Howard News

There is no better reverse mortgage information source than this one.

San Francisco Examiner

Covers the pros and cons . . . shows how to give good consideration to a reverse mortgage offer.

Senior Voice

Your
New Retirement
Nest Egg

A Consumer Guide
to the
New Reverse Mortgages

by Ken Scholen

NCHEC Press
National Center for Home Equity Conversion
Apple Valley, Minnesota

MAI *340 7451*

First Printing 1995

Printed and bound in the United States of America

All proceeds from the sale of this book support the work of the
National Center for Home Equity Conversion, an independent,
not-for-profit (501-C-3) organization (see page 334).

Library of Congress Catalog Card Number: 94-069508

ISBN 0-9630119-3-6

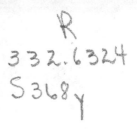

To
Sister Mary Virginia
whose prayers were answered

Table of Contents

Part
ONE

Nest Egg
Basics

Chapter 1

Your New Nest Egg

Do you own a home?

If you do, you have a retirement nest egg that you didn't have just a few years ago. Even if you've owned your home for a long time, it has only recently become a true retirement nest egg.

This book tells you why. It tells you what has happened to make your home much more valuable to you as a source of retirement income.

But more importantly, it will help you *understand* the new financial choices you now have. It will help you *make better decisions* about using - or not using - your new retirement nest egg.

The Old Hard Shell

A "nest egg" is money you keep in reserve for the future. It can also be something of value that you could turn into cash if you really need it.

Some people *have* used their homes as retirement nest eggs. But to do so, they have had to do things that most of us would rather not do:

✓ sell our homes and move elsewhere, or

✓ take out a loan against our homes, and start making monthly loan repayments.

Until recently, these were the only ways you could get cash from your home. If you were not willing to leave your home or take on new loan payments, you simply could not use the cash value of your home.

Neither Movers Nor Borrowers

But most of us want to stay in our homes and avoid debt - for good reasons.

We've put a lot of ourselves into our homes. We know them well. They shelter us and hold many wonderful memories. We like being independent. We like our homes and our neighborhoods. There's simply no place else we'd rather be.

So we don't sell and move. No matter how much cash it would put in our pockets. It's just not worth having to give up our homes.

4

And most of us don't borrow against the money value or "equity" in our homes, either. We don't like the obligation of loan payments. It's another monthly bill to pay. And it puts us at risk. If we were to miss a payment, we could lose our homes.

Besides, we worked hard to pay off a mortgage. Now that we're free of monthly loan payments, we're not looking to start making them all over again.

Too Hard to Crack

So we stay put, and do the best we can.

For most of us, home equity is not a source of retirement income at all. We spend decades building up equity in our homes. But we never cash in on our most important investment. We never get to use the equity we've worked so hard for.

If we think about using home equity at all, most of us do so with dread. As in,

☐ "I hope I never have to sell and move," or

☐ "I hope I never have to make mortgage payments again."

So we don't use our most important asset. And we even hope that we never have to! That's not much of a nest egg. That's a nest egg with a very hard shell.

So hard for most of us that our home equity remains locked up in our homes. It's ours, but we don't know any good way to get at it.

5

The New Soft Shell

Now there is a new way to turn home equity into retirement income.

A new type of loan called a "reverse" mortgage gives you cash, but requires *no monthly repayments*. In most reverse mortgages, no repayment is required *for as long as you live in your home.*

Reverse mortgages let you do something that no previous generation of Americans could do: get cash from your home without selling it, and without having to make monthly loan payments.

Reverse mortgages turn your home equity into a true retirement nest egg: a practical source of cash when you don't want to move, and don't want the burden of repaying a loan each month. *Your new retirement nest egg is the cash you could get from a "reverse" mortgage.*

For Retirees

For retired homeowners, reverse mortgages can meet a variety of needs, for example,

✓ paying off debts,

✓ dealing with financial emergencies,

✓ making home repairs or improvements,

✓ paying property taxes,

✓ increasing your monthly income,

✓ paying for help around the home,

✓ helping your children or grandchildren,

✓ giving you a cash reserve for future needs,

✓ paying for health care.

Reverse mortgages are worth something to you even if you aren't using one. Just knowing you can get at your equity if you need it - without selling your home or making loan payments - gives you more financial choices.

You do have a nest egg. You may not be using it now, and you may never use it. But knowing it's there gives you more security and flexibility. You now have a workable way to get at the equity in your home.

For Pre-Retirees

For middle-aged homeowners, reverse mortgages present a new factor in pre-retirement planning. They turn your home equity into a kind of cash reserve.

That makes your home worth more to you because you can do more than live in it. You also can use it to supplement your future retirement income.

Reverse mortgages make putting money into a home more like putting money into retirement savings. In the past, there was a sharper difference between the two. In middle age, you might have spent less money on buying or improving a home so that you could put more into retirement savings.

But now - with the availability of reverse mortgages - you might spend more on buying or improving a home because it will increase the cash you could get some day from a reverse mortgage. (In addition, you get to live in a nicer home!)

New Opportunities

In just the past few years, reverse mortgages have taken several giant steps forward. The new generation of these loans serves a much wider range of consumer needs. And they are much more widely available.

All of this is good news for consumers. It means you are increasingly likely to find a reverse mortgage that meets your individual needs. There are fewer limits on how much money you can get, and more ways in which your equity can be paid to you.

More companies are entering the market, and there is greater competition for your business. Large, well-known companies are now offering a variety of reverse mortgage products.

More new plans - previewed in this book - are about to become available soon.

New Risks

But new opportunities bring new risks.

The primary risk with reverse mortgages is that you might make a decision before you really understand how they work, what they can do, what they can't do, how much they cost, how to compare them, and how to tailor them to your individual needs.

After all, no one you know has ever done this before. These new loans are quite different from other forms of debt. Comparing reverse mortgages can be complicated. And very few professional advisors have any experience with them.

Misunderstanding can lead to mistakes. And no one can afford to make a mistake with their home equity. There's too much at stake.

That's why you need to do your homework before putting your home equity to work. To get the most out of your new retirement nest egg, you need to understand it. And that means understanding the ins and outs, and the pros and cons of reverse mortgages.

This Book

This book will help you understand, analyze, and shop for reverse mortgages - especially the new plans that have just become available, or are expected to become available soon.

9

Chapter 2 introduces you to the general concept of reverse mortgages. It presents their basic features, compares them to other loans, and describes the major types of reverse mortgages.

Chapters 3-8 show you how to analyze a reverse mortgage by breaking it down into its main parts: what you get, what you pay, and what is left when the loan is repaid. **Chapter 9** discusses other factors affecting the risks and rewards of these loans.

Part TWO (Chapters 10-18) takes you on a plan-by-plan tour of specific reverse mortgage products. It applies the analytic methods discussed in Chapters 3-9 to the full range of public and private sector programs.

Part THREE (Chapters 19-27) helps you shop for reverse mortgages. It shows you other options that may be better suited to your situation. It discusses the basic issues involved in reverse mortgage borrowing. Then it compares in detail how the different plans might meet your needs. **Part THREE** concludes with a final list of things to watch out for.

Getting Started

Even if you are already very familiar with reverse mortgages, be sure at least to scan **Part ONE.** It introduces important new concepts relating to annuities, creditlines, and cost analysis.

Part ONE will give you the background you need to understand the details presented and analyzed in **Parts TWO** and **THREE.**

Chapter 2

A New Kind Of Loan

In general, a reverse mortgage is a loan against your home that you don't have to pay back for as long as you live there.

It's a loan that can be paid to you in a several ways:

✓ a single lump sum of cash;

✓ a monthly cash advance;

✓ a "creditline" that lets you decide how much cash to get, and when to get it; or

✓ a combination of these payment methods.

The *Real* Home Equity Loan

Reverse mortgages are different from "home equity loans" in three important ways:

☐ you don't need to have a certain amount of monthly income to qualify for a reverse mortgage;

☐ you don't have to make monthly repayments on a reverse mortgage; and

☐ reverse mortgage lenders can only look to your home's value for repayment.

"Home equity" means the value of your home minus any debt against it. But so-called "home equity loans" are primarily loans against your *income*.

That's why a home equity lender checks your income - to make sure you have enough to make your monthly repayments. If you don't have enough, you won't be able to get the loan in the first place.

If you do qualify for a home equity loan, you must be certain you will be able to afford the monthly repayments. If you fall behind, the lender can foreclose and sell your home to get repaid.

Reverse mortgages, by contrast, are truly loans against home equity - and home equity *only*. They typically require no repayment until you die, sell your home, or permanently move away.

Reverse versus Forward

You can see how a reverse mortgage works by comparing it to a "forward" mortgage - the kind you use to buy a home.

Falling Debt, Rising Equity

So return with me now to those thrilling days of yesteryear when you purchased your first home. Remember?

You scraped together a down payment and borrowed the rest of the money. The loan you took out seemed like a lot, and the monthly payments probably did too.

Now think about what happened during the years that you paid back that mortgage:

◆ your debt went down, and

◆ your home equity went up.

As you made each monthly payment to the lender, the amount you owed (your "loan balance") got smaller. But your ownership value (your "equity") got larger. When you made the final mortgage payment, you owed nothing, and your home equity equaled the value of your home.

In short, you could say that a forward mortgage is a **"falling debt, rising equity"** type of deal.

Chart 1 shows how the debt falls and the equity rises in a forward mortgage. The bars show the value of a home growing over time. The shaded lower part of each bar shows the amount of debt against the home decreasing as the loan is repaid. The unshaded upper part of each bar shows the equity growing as the debt decreases and the home's value grows.

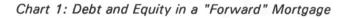

Chart 1: Debt and Equity in a "Forward" Mortgage

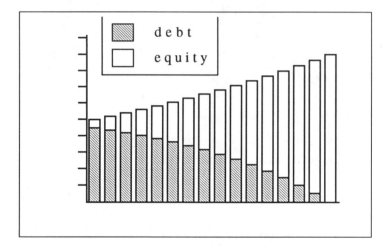

Rising Debt, Falling Equity

Reverse mortgages have different purposes than forward mortgages do. With a forward mortgage, you are using debt to build up equity in a home. But with a reverse mortgage, you are using debt to turn that equity into cash.

So here's what happens with a reverse mortgage:

◆ your debt goes up, and

◆ your home equity goes down.

It's just the opposite, or reverse, of what happens in a forward mortgage. During a reverse mortgage, the lender sends you cash, and you make no repayments. So the amount you owe gets *larger* as you get more cash and interest is added to you loan balance. This means that your equity gets *smaller* - unless your home's value is growing at a very fast rate.

When a reverse mortgage becomes due and payable, you may owe a lot of money and your equity may be very small. If you live a long time in your home, or if your home's value decreases, there may not be *any* remaining equity at the end of the loan.

In short, you could say that a reverse mortgage is a **"rising debt, falling equity"** type of deal. But that is exactly what reverse mortgage borrowers want - to "spend down" their home equity while they live in their homes without having to make loan repayments.

Chart 2 shows how the debt rises and the equity falls in a typical reverse mortgage. Again, the bars show the value of a home growing over time. But the shaded lower part of each bar shows the debt rising as the borrower receives cash (each month, in this example) and makes no repayment. The unshaded upper part of each bar shows the equity decreasing over time as the debt rises.

15

Chart 2: Debt and Equity in a Reverse Mortgage

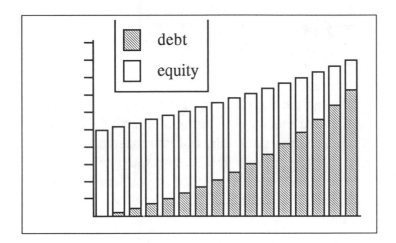

Exceptions

But does a reverse mortgage *always* have rising debt and falling equity? Look at **Chart 2** and ask yourself what would happen if the home's value grows *much faster* than the assumed 4% annual appreciation rate used in the chart.

The debt would still rise at the same rate, so the shaded lower part of the bars would be the same. But if the home's overall value grew at 8%, for example, the unshaded equity part of each bar would actually be *increasing* over time.

Chart 2 assumes that interest is being charged on regular monthly loan advances. What do you think would happen if the loan had no interest charges and consisted of a single lump sum of cash?

In that case, the loan balance would not rise. It would stay the same because nothing would be added to the original lump sum advance. This type of reverse mortgage (which is made by some government agencies, as discussed in **Part TWO**) is actually a "flat debt, rising equity" type of deal.

So there are exceptions to the general rule that reverse mortgages have rising debt and falling equity. In general, however, most loans charge interest and most home values don't grow at high rates - especially over longer periods of time.

Other Common Features

There are several different types of reverse mortgages. But they are all the same in certain ways. Here are the features that all of them have in common.

Owning Your Home

Taking out a reverse mortgage does not mean that the lender "gets" your home. You remain the owner of your home just like when you take out a forward mortgage. This means *you are responsible* for paying your property taxes and homeowner insurance, and for making property repairs.

When the loan is over, you or your heirs must repay all your cash advances and the interest that's been charged on them. Lenders don't want your house; they want their money.

Financing Your Fees

You can use money from a reverse mortgage to pay for the various fees that are charged on the loan. This is called "financing" the loan costs.

The costs are added to your loan balance, and you pay them back plus interest when the loan is over. In some programs there are limits on which or how much of these costs can be financed.

Figuring Your Cash

The amount of money you can get from a reverse mortgage depends mostly on the specific program you choose and the kind of cash advances you select.

But it also depends on your age, your home equity, and the cost of the loan. In general, *the greatest loan advances are paid to the oldest homeowners with the most home equity, and the lowest loan costs.*

Paying Your Old Debt

All reverse mortgages must be "first" mortgages. This means there can be no prior debt against your home. So if you now owe any debt on your property, you generally must do one of two things:

◆ pay off the old debt *before* you get the reverse mortgage; or

◆ pay off the old debt *with* the money you get from the reverse mortgage.

18

Capping Your New Debt

The debt you will someday owe on most reverse mortgages equals all the loan advances you receive (including any used to finance loan costs) plus all the interest that is added to your loan balance.

If that amount is *less* than your home is worth when you pay back the loan, then you or your estate get to keep whatever amount is left over.

But if your rising loan balance ever grows to *equal* the value of your home, your total debt is limited by the value of your home. Put another way, *you can never owe more than what your home is worth at the time the loan must be repaid.*

A "Non-Recourse" Loan

This overall cap on your loan balance is called a *"non-recourse"* limit. It means that the lender does not have legal recourse to anything other than your home's value. The lender may not, for example, seek repayment from your income, other assets, or heirs.

In most plans this limit is defined as the "net proceeds" from the eventual sale of your home. In some it is a fixed percentage of your home's value that you select at closing.

Managing the Risk

Let's see, now: there's no repayment required for as long as you live in your home, and you can never owe more than your home is worth. Plus, you can keep getting loan advances for as long as you live in your home, or for as long as you live anywhere.

Sounds good. But it also sounds risky for a lender, doesn't it? After all, if you live to be 105 and your home goes down in value, the lender could lose a lot of money on your loan. Right?

So how do lenders manage this risk? In one or both of two ways:

◆ the dollar amount of the loan advances is "risk-adjusted," and

◆ an insurance premium or other "risk-pooling" fee is paid by all borrowers.

Risk-Adjusting

"Risk-adjusting" means limiting the amount of money paid to borrowers based on various risk factors. Limiting the amount of the loan advances reduces the risk of loan losses.

For example, advances are usually limited to a percent of the home's value, and further limited by the borrower's age. Younger borrowers (with longer to live, on average) get smaller cash advances; older borrowers (with shorter to live) get larger advances.

Risk-Pooling

Charging insurance premiums or other similar fees on all loans creates a "risk pool" to cover the losses that do occur.

When borrowers die early or homes appreciate a lot, there are no loan losses. So the premiums on these loans can be used to cover the loan losses that occur when borrowers are long-lived or homes depreciate.

Insurance premiums and other risk-pooling fees may be financed with the loan. In some cases, the fee is used to purchase an annuity that provides monthly cash advances for the rest of a borrower's life.

You'll learn much more about these matters in later chapters. For now, just remember that the cash advances are risk-adjusted, and there may be a risk-pooling fee.

Reverse Mortgage Types

The different types of reverse mortgages can be grouped in various ways - according to who offers them, the benefits they provide, and the costs they charge.

Some are offered by private lenders such as banks, mortgage companies, savings associations, and credit unions. Others are offered by public lenders such as state and local government agencies.

A second way to categorize reverse mortgages is by their usefulness. Most are *multi-purpose* loans providing a variety of cash advance options that can be used for any purpose. But some reverse mortgages must be used for specific purposes, or are best suited to special situations.

A third way to group these loans is by the types of costs they charge. Some charge the same types of itemized costs you find on most forward mortgages. Others add an insurance premium or other risk-pooling charge. Still others base your debt on any increases in the value of your home during the loan, or on its value when the loan becomes due and payable.

Which reverse mortgage - if any - is best for you? It depends largely on your specific income needs, of course. But it also depends on how well an individual reverse mortgage program *meets* your needs. And on how much it costs. In **Part TWO**, you will learn all about these programs one by one.

Up Next

But first, the next chapter shows you an overall approach to analyzing reverse mortgages of all kinds. The remainder of **Part ONE** then explains this method in greater detail. It shows you what to ask, what to look for, and what to look out for.

Chapter 3

Three Basic Questions

A reverse mortgage turns your home equity into three things:

◆ **cash advances** paid to you,

◆ **loan costs** paid to the lender, and

◆ **leftover cash**, if any, paid to you or your heirs at the end of the loan.

Since reverse mortgages turn home equity into three things, you can analyze any reverse mortgage by asking three simple questions:

☐ What do you get?

☐ What do you pay?

☐ What would be left at the end of the loan?

It's especially important that you ask *all three* questions. You may prefer getting as much money as possible. But what if a plan paying you a *little* more money has a *much higher* price tag? Or what if a plan paying just a *little* less money or costing just a *little* more left you with *a lot more* equity?

You can't choose the program that best meets your needs if you don't fully understand it. And to do that, you must look at the full picture.

Coming Up

The rest of **Part ONE** takes a closer look at each of the questions listed above.

◆ **Chapter 4** considers the types and amounts of cash *benefits* that reverse mortgages provide.

◆ **Chapters 5-7** show that the real *cost* of these loans is much different than you might expect.

◆ **Chapter 8** discusses *what's left* at the end of a reverse mortgage.

◆ And **Chapter 9** presents program-specific factors that can affect a reverse mortgage's benefits, cost, and leftover cash.

Chapter 4

Cash Benefits

You're probably most interested in *how much* money can you get from a reverse mortgage. But you also need to find out *what kind* of money you can get.

Different reverse mortgage programs offer different types of cash advances.

☐ Some plans offer several choices or combinations of cash advance types.

☐ Other plans require that the money must be paid to you in a certain way, or used by you in a certain way.

The basic types of cash advances are lump sums, creditlines, and monthly advances.

Lump Sums

Some reverse mortgage programs let you take all the money available to you at once in a single "lump sum" of cash.

This is typically done on the day you sign all the papers for "closing" your loan. The lender gives you a check for a large amount of money, and that's it. You are not eligible for any more cash advances.

In some plans you can combine a lump sum at closing with a creditline or monthly advance. But that reduces the amount of the lump sum. In plans that require a monthly cash advance, there are usually limits on how much of a lump sum you can get.

Creditlines

Some reverse mortgage programs let you put all the money available to you into a "creditline" - which is also known as a "line-of-credit."

A creditline is a personal account that you control. You decide when to take money out, and how much money to take out. So it works pretty much like a checking account. But the cash you get from a creditline is a *loan* that creates debt against your home.

Instead of choosing a creditline, you might be tempted to take out a lump sum of cash and put it into a savings or money market account.

Yes, you would earn interest on such accounts. But you have to look at the costs as well.

Remember, you also would be *charged* interest on the *full amount* of any lump sum. And the interest rate on the lump sum would undoubtedly be *greater* than the rate you could earn on any low-risk account. So the result would be a net interest cost to you.

With a creditline, on the other hand, you are only charged interest on the cash advances you actually receive. You are not charged interest on the overall creditline amount that is available to you.

Flat versus Growing

Some creditlines are flat, and some grow. The difference is an important one, because it affects how much money you can get.

For example, if a creditline of $50,000 is "flat," you can never get more than $50,000 from it. If it is "growing," however, you *can* get more than $50,000. How much more depends on the rate at which it grows, and when you take the money out.

If it grows by 5% per year, for example, and you don't take any cash advances over the first year of the loan, you could get $52,500 at the end of the first year ($50,000 + 5%). If you wait five years before using it, you could get $63,814 at that time.

Due to the cost of setting up a reverse mortgage, though, it's generally not a good idea to take a creditline if you don't intend to use it for a while.

But these examples show how important a growing creditline can be. When you do take cash advances, the lender generally subtracts your rising balance (including interest) from your growing creditline to determine how much credit is left.

But if your creditline is flat, your cash advances are subtracted from a fixed creditline. So you're more likely to run out of money sooner.

Monthly Advances

Monthly loan advances are fixed cash payments made to you by check or directly deposited in your checking account each month. The different types of monthly loan advances vary by *how long* the lender agrees to make the advances:

◆ **term** advances continue for a fixed period of time that you select at loan closing;

◆ **tenure** advances continue for as long as you live in your home;

◆ **lifetime** advances continue for as long as you live - *wherever* you live.

Term advances, which usually run for the shortest length of time, are generally larger in dollar amount than tenure or lifetime advances. The shorter the term you select, the larger the monthly advances will be.

In most loans providing term advances, the mortgage does not become due and payable when the loan advances stop. In some plans, however, it does.

Tenure advances give you long-term income security. No matter how long you live, no matter what happens to the value of your home, you continue getting fixed monthly advances until you die, sell your home, or permanently move away.

Lifetime advances provide even greater income security. These advances continue every month even if you sell or move. But the structure of these plans may raise other issues for you to consider.

Reverse <u>Annuity</u> Mortgages

Lifetime advances can be guaranteed by combining a reverse mortgage with an *annuity*.

A lump sum advance from the loan is typically used to purchase an annuity in your name. An annuity is a contract from a life insurance company to pay you a fixed amount of money every month for the rest of your life.

But these are annuity advances. And unlike loan advances, annuity advances are partially taxable. And they also may make you ineligible for - or sharply reduce your cash benefits from - various government programs.

In the Supplemental Security Income (SSI) program, for example, annuity advances can reduce your benefits dollar-for-dollar.

31

So you need to look at how much money you would get from a reverse annuity mortgage on a "net" basis - that is, after taxes and after any public benefit reductions. Although you may not be eligible for these programs now, you might need them later.

You also need to be concerned about the safety and security of any annuity. Life insurance companies can and do fail. So you should be certain that your annuity comes from a company with strong financial ratings (more on this in **Chapter 9**).

Reverse annuity lenders should give you at least two life insurance companies to choose between. Companies with stronger ratings may provide smaller annuity advances. So you might have to choose between having greater security and less cash, or greater cash and less security.

Just remember, a reverse *annuity* mortgage can be more complicated that a reverse mortgage. So take the time you need to consider the additional issues these programs present.

Combinations

Many reverse mortgages let you combine different types of loan advances. As mentioned earlier, just about all plans let you take some kind of lump sum at closing.

And in some plans you can combine a creditline with a lump sum or monthly advance. But that reduces the amount of the creditline. In plans that require a monthly loan advance, there are usually limits on how much of a creditline you can get.

If you are interested in a monthly advance, you should give serious consideration to including a creditline if possible. Although this reduces your monthly advance, it gives you greater flexibility for meeting unexpected or irregular expenses. It also gives you some protection against inflation.

Those fixed monthly loan advances might look awfully good to you today. But how will they look after five, ten, or 15 years of inflation? They certainly won't buy as much then.

So you might be better off overall taking a lesser monthly advance now plus a creditline. In that way you can supplement your monthly advance in the future. If the creditline grows each year, you would have an even stronger hedge against rising prices.

Loan Advance Amounts

The amount of money you can get from a reverse mortgage depends on several factors.

The total amount available to you depends on the specific reverse mortgage program you select. Within each program, the funds available to you are generally determined by three main factors: your age, your home equity, and the cost of your loan.

Most programs then let you decide how to split up your total available cash. In other words, they let you choose how much of your money you'll get through which types of advances.

Three Main Factors

The older you are at closing, the more money you can get in most plans. If you are a "joint" borrower (that is, if your spouse or some other person co-owns your home), some programs simply use the age of the youngest borrower. Others use actuarial formulas to "blend" your ages.

The more equity you have, the more money you can get. But most plans place minimum or maximum limits on the amount of equity they will lend against. So you might get more money from one program than from another because their limits are different, or because one has limits and the other doesn't.

The more the loan costs, the less money you can get. As you will soon learn, the real, total cost of a reverse mortgage is not as obvious as it might appear to be. But if more of your equity goes to the lender to cover loan costs, less will be available to you in the form of cash advances.

Allocating Your Funds

The amount of money you can get from a reverse mortgage depends on how and when you decide to have it paid to you.

Under a plan insured by the federal government, for example, you can choose from among a wide range of options.

If you are a 75-year-old living in a debt-free home valued at $100,000, and the expected interest rate on the loan is 9%, here are some of the approximate choices you would have in this plan:

☐ $38,000 in a single lump sum of cash; or

☐ $38,000 in a creditline (that grows by 9.5% each year); or

☐ a $10,000 lump sum and a $28,000 creditline; or

☐ $330 per month for as long as you live in your home; or

☐ $790 per month for 5 years, $490/month for 10 years, or $395/month for 15 years; or

☐ a $5,000 lump sum and a $10,000 creditline and $240 per month for 15 years.

These examples show you the types of choices you have. In fact, you can allocate your money among the different types of cash advances in just about any way you want in this program.

Just remember, putting more of your equity into one type of cash advance leaves less for the others.

Benefits versus Costs

In analyzing any reverse mortgage, you need to learn

✓ what types of cash advances it provides, and

✓ how much money you can get in each type of cash advance.

But you also need to know how much a reverse mortgage costs. That's the focus of the next three chapters.

◆ **Chapter 5** looks at the individual, *itemized costs* that are often charged on reverse mortgages.

◆ **Chapter 6** shows you how the *total cost* of these loans is calculated.

◆ **Chapter 7** helps you *evaluate* reverse mortgage costs.

Chapter 5

Itemized Costs

Do you want to know what reverse mortgages *really* cost? Do you want to know the *total* cost of these loans? Do you want to be able to compare the cost of different *types* of reverse mortgages?

If you do, you will *not* find the answers in this chapter.

Instead, you will learn about all the individual, itemized costs that are generally charged on these loans. And that will prepare you to learn about the real, total cost of reverse mortgages in **Chapters 6** and **7**.

The Itemized Approach

The traditional way of evaluating loan costs is to look at individual cost items one at a time.

This "itemized" approach provides important and essential information. It is normally the only advance information you get on forward mortgages.

But this information alone does not show you the *total* cost of a reverse mortgage. On loans with complex costs, this approach can be more confusing than helpful. Some lenders do not even use traditional itemized charges in calculating the cost of their loans.

Different Costs

The methods used to figure out how much you owe on a reverse mortgage can be quite different from the ones used on forward mortgages.

More important, the types of costs can vary a lot from one reverse mortgage plan to another. **Table 1** shows you just how different these costs can be. It is based on real programs you will learn more about in **Part TWO**.

Don't get too discouraged when you look at the different types of costs in **Table 1**. The traditional itemized approach can be very confusing when applied to these new kinds of loans.

That's why the next chapter will introduce you to a new approach.

Table 1: Types of Costs on Reverse Mortgages

Program A	- an origination fee that varies by lender - an adjustable interest rate subject to annual and overall caps - an insurance premium charged in 2 parts: a per cent of home value at closing (subject to limits that vary by location); and a fixed add-on to the interest rate charged on the loan balance
Program B	- total amount owed at end of loan is a per cent of the home's value at that time - the per cent is selected by you at closing; it determines how much money you get - exception # 1: if your home's value goes down, there is a minimum repayment - exception #2: if you repay the loan early, you pay the minimum plus a fixed rate of annual interest on that amount
Program C	- an origination fee based on home value at closing - a maturity fee based on home value at the end of the loan - a fixed interest rate charged on lump sum and monthly advances - a different fixed rate charged on creditline advances - the cost of a deferred annuity - up to one-half of any increase in the home's value during the loan

The new way of evaluating loan costs is concerned only with the *total cost* of the loan. But for now, let's take a quick and closer look at the different types of *itemized costs* charged on reverse mortgages.

Item by Item

Some of the itemized costs in this section will be familiar to you. They are basically the same as the ones charged on most forward mortgages. But others may be completely unfamiliar. So read carefully.

Origination Fees

Origination fees pay lenders for preparing all the paperwork and processing your loan. This is also called "originating" or setting up your loan.

Closing Costs

Completing a mortgage transaction - also known as "closing" a loan - requires a variety of services by third parties other than the originating lender. These services include appraisals, title search and insurance, surveys, inspections, recording fees, mortgage taxes, credit checks, and others.

Closing costs vary with home values. They also can vary tremendously from one area to another. But all the lenders in any state or local area are likely to charge about the same closing costs on a given loan.

Servicing Fees

"Servicing" a loan means everything lenders do after originating a loan: making cash advances, sending account statements, paying property taxes and insurance from the loan at your request, arranging the purchase of an annuity, checking to see that you comply with your obligations under the loan agreement.

Sometimes these services are not performed by the same company that originates the loan. An originating lender that transfers servicing to another company must give you the name, address, and phone number of a contact person with the servicer.

Servicing fees can be included in the interest rate charged on your loan balance or charged as a separate fee on a monthly basis.

Interest

Interest rates can be either fixed or adjustable. A fixed rate never changes. An adjustable rate usually starts out being lower than a fixed rate. But it can increase or decrease at times and within limits specified in the loan agreement. The more adjustable the rate is, the lower the beginning rate is likely to be.

Generally lenders have no control over interest rate adjustments. Rate changes are simply tied to movements in well-known interest rate indexes published by major newspapers.

Once the loan begins, however, rate changes generally do not affect your cash advances. You continue to get the same monthly advances and your "gross" creditline does not change or continues to grow at the rate specified in the loan agreement.

What does change is the rate at which your loan balance grows: faster if interest rates increase, slower if rates decrease. And this affects how much equity will be left at the end of your loan. It also may affect how much will be left in your "net" creditline.

Risk-Pooling Fees

As discussed in **Chapter 2**, the risk of loan losses may be covered by an insurance premium or other risk-pooling fee.

It may be charged as a percentage of home value at closing, as an annual fee tied to the loan balance or the home's value, or both. In some cases, the risk-pooling fee takes the form of an annuity premium or guaranty fee.

Appreciation Sharing

Some reverse mortgages include a cost related to any increases in the value of your home (that is, any appreciation) that occurs during the loan. When the loan is over, the lender is owed some agreed-upon percentage of any increase in the value of the property since loan closing.

For example, if your home is worth $100,000 at closing and $150,000 when the loan ends, its value has appreciated by $50,000. If you had agreed to pay 50% "shared appreciation," you could owe the lender as much as $25,000 on this cost item alone.

Shared appreciation is generally charged *in addition to* a fixed rate of interest on the loan advances. This gives the loan a kind of overall variable rate.

"Percent of Value" Pricing

The total amount owed on some reverse mortgages is based on a percentage of the value of your home when the loan becomes due and payable.

You select the percentage - generally ranging from 25% to 75% - at loan closing. The greater the percentage you choose, the greater your cash advances will be.

Loans with "percent of value" pricing (also known as "equity sharing") can be *extremely expensive* in the short run. For example, *you could owe up to 75% of your home's value after only a few years.* But these loans also can end up being quite inexpensive if you outlive your life expectancy.

Confusing Costs

As you saw in **Table 2,** the itemized approach shows you only the various pieces of the cost puzzle. It generally doesn't give you the total cost, and that makes it very difficult to compare one loan with another.

The itemized approach only tells you what is going to be charged on your loan. It generally doesn't tell you what you are likely to end up actually paying.

So how can you tell the real, total cost of a reverse mortgage? **Chapter 6** awaits you.

Chapter **6**

Total Costs

You have now come to the most important chapter in this book.

It's pretty easy to figure out "what you can get" from a reverse mortgage. "What you really pay" is a bit trickier.

But you need to know what you are paying for these new types of loans. Even if it might take a little extra effort to understand.

So take your time with **Chapter 6**. It includes important and essential information. You'll need it later when we compare the cost of different plans.

A Tale of Two Borrowers

You can see how to calculate the real, total cost of a reverse mortgage by following a simple example of two reverse mortgage borrowers:

✓ Lucy and Monica are neighbors of the same age living in identical homes worth $100,000. They take out reverse mortgages from the same lender on the same day.

✓ The interest rate on each loan is a flat 9%.

✓ The start-up cost (origination, closing, and risk-pooling fee) for each loan totals $5,000 - and both borrowers finance it.

Same Total Cost?

With the same interest rate and the same start-up cost, you would think that the total cost of each loan would be the same. Right?

In fact, the total cost of these loans is very unlikely to be the same. As you follow the example of Lucy and Monica, you will learn why this is so. You also will find out what factors affect the true, total cost of these loans.

You might not believe that a borrower's *name* could affect the cost of her loan. But did you know that the full names of the neighbors in our example are Lucy Lump Sum and Monica Monthly?

Choices and Time

In fact, the cash advance choices that a borrower makes do affect the real cost of the loan.

Lucy and Monica are each given the choice of a lump sum or creditline of $35,000 - or a monthly advance of $350. True to her somewhat unusual name, Lucy takes the lump sum, and Monica - surprising no one - takes the monthly advance.

So now, which borrower will pay more for her loan? You still don't have enough information to tell. For the real, total cost of a reverse mortgage also depends on how long the loan runs.

To see how cash advance choices and the length of the loan affect its cost, let's look in on Lucy and Monica two years after they take out their loans.

Two Years Later

Table 2 shows that after two years Lucy Lump Sum has received $35,000 in cash and owes $12,857 in loan costs for a total debt of $47,856.

Monica Monthly has received $8,400 ($350 a month for two years) and owes $6,817 in loan costs for a total debt of $15,217.

So Monica owes fewer total dollars, and the dollar amount of her loan costs is less. *But she also got a lot less cash from the deal.*

So did she pay more or less than Lucy for the money she actually got?

Table 2: Two Borrowers - Two Years Later

	Lucy Lump Sum	Monica Monthly
Total Cash Received	**$35,000** lump sum at loan closing	$350/month for 2 years (**$8,400**)
Start-Up Costs	$5,000	$5,000
Total Interest at 9%	$7,857	$1,817
Total Loan Costs	**$12,857**	**$6,817**
Total Amount Owed	**$47,857**	**$15,217**
Total Loan Cost Rate	15.7%	53.8%

Total Loan Cost Rates

To find the total cost of these loans, you need to combine all the loan costs into a Total Loan Cost (TLC) rate. This is the annual average rate that would generate the total amount owed at any point during the loan if it had been charged on the cash advances made prior to that point.

Simply put, the TLC is the annual average rate that includes *all* the costs of a reverse mortgage. If the total cost had to be generated by a single interest rate charged on the cash advances only, that single, all-inclusive rate would be the TLC.

The advantage of the TLC method is that it shows you the *total* cost of the loan. It combines *all* the itemized costs into a single figure.

You can even use the TLC method on loans without traditional itemized costs. All you need to know is the total amount owed, the cash advances received by the borrower, and the length of the loan term.

You just punch this information into a hand-held financial calculator, and it computes the TLC for you (see **Appendix A** for more details).

In our example, if the loan ends after two years, Lucy ends up paying a TLC rate of 15.7% on her lump sum. But Monica pays 53.8% per year on her monthly advances.

Why So Much?

TLC rates are generally greater than the rate actually charged on the loan balance because they include that rate PLUS all the other loan costs.

On any reverse mortgage, the TLC is greatest in the early years of the loan because the start-up costs are spread out over only a few years.

In the short term, TLC rates are especially high on loans with monthly advances. That's because the total amount of cash you get is much less than most lump sums. You get less money, but the start-up costs are the same. You can see how this works in the case of Lucy Lump Sum and Monica Monthly.

Lump Sum versus Monthly

The reason Monica's TLC rate is so much higher than Lucy's is that her total dollar costs ($6,817) are a greater part of her total debt ($15,217) than Lucy's are. By contrast, Lucy's total dollar costs ($12,857) are a smaller part of her total debt ($47,857) than Monica's are.

In other words, Monica pays $6,817 in loan costs for $8,400 in monthly advances over two years. So her TLC rate is very high. You have to charge 53.8% annual interest (4.4855% per month) on $350 each month for two years to get a total debt of $15,217.

Lucy, by contrast, pays $12,857 in loan costs for a $35,000 lump sum advance. So her TLC rate is much less. If you charge 15.7% annual interest (1.3121% per month) on $35,000 for two years, the total debt will equal $47,857.

Now let's see what happens to the TLC rates if the loans run longer than two years.

Less Costly Over Time

TLC rates generally get smaller over time for two reasons. As your rising debt grows

◆ your start-up costs become a smaller part of your total debt, and

◆ your total debt may catch up to - and then be limited by - the value of your home.

As the start-up costs are spread out over more and more years, they become a smaller and smaller part of your total debt. This makes the TLC on your loan get smaller over time.

Non-Recourse Lowers TLC

The other reason TLC rates drop over time is that rising loan balances are limited by home values.

Remember, the non-recourse limit on these loans means you can never owe more than the value of your home. In most plans that means the net proceeds from the eventual sale of your home. In others, your debt is limited to a fixed per cent of your home's value.

In any case, if your rising loan balance reaches your non-recourse limit, your debt will be capped thereafter by that limit.

When this happens, the TLC rate on your loan starts dropping at a faster rate. The more slowly your home grows in value, the more likely this is to occur, and the faster your TLC will drop.

If your home appreciates at a fast rate, by contrast, it is much less likely that your loan balance will rise fast enough to catch up to the value of your home.

Lump Sum versus Monthly

TLC rates on monthly advances come down much faster than TLCs on lump sums. If you live long enough, and your home appreciates moderately or less, the TLC rate on monthly advances can become smaller than the TLC on lump sums.

Table 3: TLCs on Lump Sum and Monthly Advances at Various Times and Annual Appreciation Rates*

	Lucy Lump Sum	Monica Monthly
TLC After 2 Years	15.7%	53.8%
TLC After 10 Years		
at 0% appreciation	9.8%	11.8%
at appreciation > 0.5%	10.3%	11.8%
TLC After 20 Years		
at 0% appreciation	4.9%	1.0%
at 3% appreciation	7.9%	6.3%
at 6% appreciation	9.7%	9.9%

Table 3 shows how this works on the loans taken out by Lucy and Monica. In general, you can see that the TLCs on both loans come down over time.

TLCs on monthly advances drop the most - from 53.8% after two years to 11.8% after 10 years to anywhere from 1.0% to 9.9% after 20 years, depending on the annual rate of appreciation.

When there is no appreciation, the TLC rate on the monthly advance after 20 years is only 1%. It's so low because the rising debt has long ago caught up to the non-recourse limit.* Ever since then, Monica has continued to receive monthly cash advances while the amount she owes has remained the same.

* In Table 3 and throughout this book, the nonrecourse limit is assumed to be the net sale proceeds (unless the program under consideration defines it differently). The net sale proceeds are assumed to be 93% of the home's value. This leaves 7% for the costs of selling the home.

If someone lended you $350 every month and at some point "froze" your debt while continuing to send you $350 each month, the real cost of you loan would drop pretty fast, too. When there is no appreciation, the non-recourse limit never increases. So once the limit is reached, the debt stops rising.

Lucy's lump sum debt reaches the non-recourse limit at 0% appreciation even sooner: after ten years. That's why her TLC rate at that point is lower at 0% appreciation than at all annual average appreciation rates greater than 0.5%.

Major Cost Factors

Which loan costs more? There's only one definitive answer: it depends. What's it depend on? As you have seen so far, the TLC rate varies with

✓ the cash advances you select,

✓ the length of your loan, and

✓ changes in the value of your property.

There are two additional cost factors that may affect the final cost of your reverse mortgage:

✓ how you use a creditline; and

✓ changes in interest and appreciation rates.

Creditline Advances

If you use most of a creditline at closing or near the beginning of the loan, the TLC pattern over time will more closely resemble the costs on a lump sum advance.

On the other hand, if you take the money in smaller amounts on a regular basis, the TLC pattern over time will more closely resemble the costs on monthly advances.

To see this more clearly, just imagine what would happen if Lucy and Monica's friend Chris Creditline took out the same reverse mortgage that they did. If Chris puts all his money into a creditline, the TLC rates on his loan will depend on how he uses it.

☐ If he takes out $34,000 one month after closing, then the TLC pattern on his loan will be very similar to the cost pattern on Lucy Lump Sum's loan.

☐ But if he takes out $4,000 each year, the TLC pattern on his loan will be very similar to the pattern on Monica Monthly's loan.

The highest TLC rates on a creditline will result if you take out no money at closing and very little for a long time after that. The total dollar amount you would owe in this case might be very low. But the real cost of the little cash you actually receive would be very high on a TLC basis.

Creditline TLC rates can vary widely depending on usage. So when comparing different programs, it's important to assume the same pattern of usage. In that way you'll be comparing apples to apples.

When calculating creditline TLCs in this book, we will assume (unless otherwise noted) that borrowers use 50% of their available credit at closing, and none after that. This is the standard assumption used for calculating TLC projections by the federally-insured reverse mortgage program.

It probably doesn't reflect how you would use your creditline. But it gives us a general usage standard by which different creditline programs can be compared.

Changing Rates

Before your loan closes, you can estimate its future TLCs based on assumptions about how long the loan will run, what will happen to your home's value, and how you will use a creditline.

With this type of projection, it is convenient to assume that interest rates and home appreciation rates will not change over time. In reality, that is not likely to be true.

But for every pattern of future rate changes there is an equivalent fixed rate. So the fixed rates used to estimate TLC rates also represent several variable rate patterns. In general, they represent an estimate of the annual average rates of interest and appreciation.

After your loan is closed, the actual TLC rate will depend on the actual pattern of interest and appreciation rate changes.

Putting TLCs To Work

Now you know how the true, total cost of any reverse mortgage can be calculated.

But how can you use this knowledge to help you evaluate and compare the costs of different programs? **Chapter 7** completes your introduction to TLC rates.

Chapter 7

Evaluating Costs

The good news is that you don't have to figure out the Total Loan Cost (TLC) rates by yourself anymore.

Recent amendments to federal Truth-In-Lending laws require lenders to provide a table of TLC rate projections for every reverse mortgage.

As this book went to press, the Federal Reserve Board was developing specific regulations to carry out the new law (see **Appendix A**).

TLC Tables

For any given reverse mortgage, the required TLC tables will show the projected TLC rate at different points in the future based on various assumptions about home appreciation.

In particular, they will show projected TLC rates after a short time, at your life expectancy, and at a point beyond your life expectancy. This will let you see the loan's overall cost pattern.

The tables will be based on the cash advances you select. If you choose a creditline, the TLCs will reflect a standard assumption about creditline usage.

Your Right to TLC

Unlike all past reverse mortgage shoppers, you have a legal right to see the TLC rates for all reverse mortgages*. And federal law now requires that every lender must calculate TLCs in exactly the same way.

---

* The TLC concept and methodology were initially developed by the National Center for Home Equity Conversion in its "Financial Guide to Reverse Mortgages" in 1989. NCHEC's method of analyzing reverse mortgage costs was then adopted by the U. S. Congress in 1990, when it required a "total loan cost" disclosure for the federally-insured Home Equity Conversion Mortgage program. In 1992, NCHEC's **Retirement Income On The House** further developed the "Total Loan Cost" (TLC) concept for evaluating loan costs.

The TLC methodology being developed by the Federal Reserve may differ somewhat from the calculations in this book. For example, it may use initial rather than expected interest rates. The basic formula and the resulting cost patterns will be the same, however (see **Appendix A**).

So the job of comparing total loan costs from one program to another will be much simpler than ever before. In **Part TWO** you will see TLC tables for each reverse mortgage program. In **Part THREE** you will see how these costs compare with each other.

For now, let's focus on the big picture. What do TLC rates tell you in general about the cost of reverse mortgages? How does this help you estimate the real, total cost of any specific reverse mortgage program you might consider?

Basic Cost Patterns

TLC rates outline the basic structure of reverse mortgage costs in general. By looking at TLC tables, you can see the underlying cost pattern for all reverse mortgages.

As you have learned, a variety of factors affect these cost patterns. But after you select your cash advances, the most important overall factor is time. In general, reverse mortgages are

✓ most costly in the short run;

✓ less costly over time; and

✓ least costly when you live longer than average and your home appreciates at a low or moderate rate.

If you live in your home only a short time after closing a reverse mortgage, the final TLC rate on your loan may be much greater than you ever imagined it could be. This is especially true if you take monthly advances only, or if you make little use of a creditline.

If you live longer than people your age normally live, the final TLC rate on your loan may be much lower than you expected it could be.

It may even drop below any interest rate actually charged on your loan balance at any time during the life of your loan. The longer you live in your home relative to your life expectancy, the more likely this is to occur.

In extreme cases - very long life plus flat or declining home values - TLCs can become *negative* in some programs. In other words, you could actually end up "earning" interest rather than paying it. This may be very unlikely, but it is possible.

More Than a Loan

So that's the basic pattern of reverse mortgage costs: potentially very expensive in the short run, less costly over time, and least expensive in the long run.

The main reason for this pattern is that a reverse mortgage is *more than a loan*. By providing ongoing cash advances while postponing all repayment, a reverse mortgage is more like a loan *plus an annuity*. It provides credit plus security over time.

Two Services In One

In some reverse mortgage programs, you actually use loan advances to purchase an annuity from a life insurance company. But no matter how they are structured, all reverse mortgages combine elements of a loan and an annuity.

This means that you are really purchasing what always used to be two different types of financial services. And each has a cost. When you combine them, the overall start-up cost is greater, but you get the combined benefit of two services.

That's why a reverse mortgage might end up costing you *much more* than a forward mortgage. But that's also why it might end up costing you *much less* than a forward mortgage.

Which will it be? After you've selected your cash advances, it depends primarily on how long you live in your home and how much its value changes during that time.

So how long *are* you likely to live in your home, and what's likely to happen to its value?

Life & Value

Neither you nor the lender can know for certain how long you will live in your home and how its value will change during that time. But you can make an educated guess.

61

In fact, you may be in a much better position to do so than any lender. After all, you know more about your health and your home than any lender does.

Estimating Life

Life expectancy tables are a good starting point for estimating how long you might live in your home. **Table 4** shows the average remaining years of life for males and females of various ages.

These averages may or may not reflect how long reverse mortgage borrowers will live. They may live longer due to increased income. Or, like annuities, reverse mortgages may prove to be more attractive to people who tend to live longer.

On the other hand, some borrowers will not live in their homes for the rest of their lives. They will sell, pay back their loans, and move elsewhere. So life expectancy may be as good a general measure as any.

Estimating Value

Future changes in home values are even trickier to estimate.

Since World War II, the national average value of family homes has generally changed each year by a bit more than the overall inflation rate in that year. But in recent years, that relationship has been less consistent.

Over the past decade, the average annual change in the value of existing single family homes nationally has ranged from about 3% to 4% - depending on the statistical method used to measure it.

Table 4: Average Remaining Years of Life for Males and Females of Various Ages

AGE	Male	Female		AGE	Male	Female
65	14.2	18.4		78	7.6	9.8
66	13.6	17.7		79	7.2	9.2
67	13.0	17.0		80	6.8	8.7
68	12.5	16.3		81	6.4	8.2
69	11.9	15.5		82	6.1	7.7
70	11.4	14.8		83	5.8	7.2
71	10.8	14.2		84	5.4	6.8
72	10.3	13.5		85	5.1	6.4
73	9.8	12.8		86	4.9	6.0
74	9.4	12.2		87	4.6	5.6
75	8.9	11.6		88	4.3	5.3
76	8.5	11.0		89	4.1	5.0
77	8.0	10.4		90	3.9	4.7

Source: National Center for Health Statistics: U.S. Decennial Life Tables for 1979-81

But national averages include a wide variety of local and regional housing markets. In some, homes are appreciating at high rates. In others, homes are depreciating in value.

How are home values changing in your area? That may be your best clue about what might happen in the short run. But just remember that today's hot market can lose its lustre, and today's declining neighborhood can rebound sharply.

To cover a range of possibilities, the tables in this book use three appreciation rates: 0%, 3%, and 6%.

The annual change in *your* home's value may be greater than 6% or less than 0% - especially in the short run. Over longer periods of time, however, it is more likely that changes in your home's value will fall within this range on an annual average basis.

Estimating Cost

So you make your best guess about how long you'll live in your home and how much its value will change during that time. For most people, life expectancy (see **Table 4**) and 3% appreciation is probably as good a starting point as any.

Look at the TLC tables for the loans you are considering:

☐ see what the real, total cost of the loans would be at 3% appreciation at your life expectancy;

☐ check what the TLC rate would be if you live in your home longer or shorter than your life expectancy; and

☐ check what the TLC would be if your home appreciates at a faster or slower rate.

This will show you the overall pattern or range of potential loan costs.

Comparing TLC Rates

TLC patterns for all the loans in any reverse mortgage program tend to be similar, assuming that the types of cash advances are the same. But TLC patterns can vary significantly from one reverse mortgage program to another, even if the types of cash advances are exactly the same.

For example, one program's monthly advances may have *much greater* TLC rates than another's in the early years of a loan, but *much lower* TLCs in the later years of the same loan. It is unusual that one program *always* has greater TLC rates than another.

Total versus Itemized

Remember, it is the TLC that shows you the true, total cost of the transaction. Do not be confused by the traditional checklist of itemized loan costs. They only tell you what a lender will charge.

The problem is that the types of charges - and the cash advance amounts - vary a lot from one program to another. Some don't even use itemized costs to determine how much you owe. And the non-recourse limit caps your debt anyhow. So it's impossible to compare total costs on an "apples to apples" basis using itemized loan charges.

TLC rates show what you will pay *in total* on an average annual basis. They reduce the complexity of widely different types and amounts of loan charges into single rates. TLCs are the only way to compare total costs on a true "side by side" basis.

TLC Limitations

TLC rates are very helpful in understanding the basic cost structure of reverse mortgages. For example, they show consumers planning to sell and move in a few years that the real cost of their loans could be very high.

TLCs are also very helpful in comparing different reverse mortgage programs. **Part THREE** will give you a full plate of such comparisons.

But there are limits to the usefulness of TLCs. And you need to understand what those limits are.

Cost versus Value

TLC rates can show you the true, total cost of a reverse mortgage. But they can't tell you what it's worth to you. Only you can do that.

The value of a reverse mortgage depends on what you get for what you pay. And only you can decide what the benefits of any reverse mortgage are worth to you.

Projected versus Real

At closing, TLCs *project* the overall pattern of cost on a reverse mortgage. But they don't tell you for certain what the actual cost of your loan will end up being. That will depend primarily on how long you live in your home and what happens to its value.

So when you compare the cost of one reverse mortgage program with another, you can only see which would cost less under various assumptions.

You might select one plan rather than another because its TLCs beyond life expectancy are much lower - and then die after three years, when the TLC rate on the plan you selected is much greater.

Always the Low Price?

Some people will do everything they can to get the lowest possible price. There are some ways of getting the lowest possible TLC, however, that don't make any sense at all.

For example, TLC rates are lowest when home values decrease. But this doesn't mean you should try to drive down the value of your property. That would only reduce the amount of equity you or your heirs would have left at the end of your loan.

The same is true for using a creditline. Yes, the TLC will be lower if you use more of it sooner. But that shouldn't lead you to being less careful with your money. The more you spend now, the less you will have in the future.

Knowing that a lump sum has lower TLCs than a monthly advance, you might be tempted to take a lump sum when what you really need is a monthly advance. This makes no sense if you intend to bank the lump sum and make monthly withdrawals, for example.

You'd end up paying much more interest on the lump sum advance than you'd ever safely earn on it - a sure plan for losing money.

Once your loan has closed, the best way to get the lowest possible TLC rate is by living longer than your life expectancy. So if you're really intent on getting the best deal, use your cash advances to take good care of yourself.

Question #3

What can you get from a reverse mortgage? In **Chapter 4,** you saw the cash benefits these loans can provide.

What does it cost? In **Chapters 5-7,** you saw how to analyze the cost of these loans.

The next chapter considers the third basic question you need to ask about any reverse mortgage: What would be left at the end of the loan?

Chapter 8

Leftover Cash

If you're like most people, you want to remain in your own home for the rest of your life. Maybe that's why you're considering a reverse mortgage. So you can afford to do so.

But what would happen if you took out a reverse mortgage, and then moved out several years later?

Moving Questions

If you move, your reverse mortgage becomes due and payable at that time. To repay the loan, you probably would have to sell your home. But what would you have left after paying off the loan?

This is an important question for several reasons:

♦ If you have to move for health reasons, you may need to pay for the cost of assisted living or other types of care.

♦ If you have already used the one-time capital gains exclusion or your projected gain would exceed your interest deductions, you may have tax obligations.

♦ In any case, you would need to pay for the cost of moving and future living expenses.

Part THREE considers these issues further. But you can see already that "What do I get?" and "What do I pay?" aren't the only financial questions you should be asking. "What would be left?" is the third basic question you need to ask.

Even if you live in your home for the rest of your life, you may want to leave a bequest for your heirs or for other purposes. So the amount of cash that's left over at the end of a reverse mortgage may be important to you even if you never move from your home.

Annuity and Equity

What's left when you pay back a reverse mortgage? Leftover cash may be available in two forms:

✓ you may receive continuing monthly advances from an annuity, and

✓ you or your estate may receive a lump sum of leftover equity.

If your reverse mortgage program includes an annuity, you would continue to receive monthly cash advances for life. If it does not, you would not get any more monthly advances.

In either case, you may or may not have leftover equity. Leftover equity is the lump sum of cash paid to you (or your estate) that is left after your debt has been repaid.

Calculating Leftovers

The amount of any leftover equity at the end of your loan depends on

◆ how much you owe,

◆ what your home is worth, and

◆ the non-recourse limit on your loan.

In most programs, your debt equals all the *loan* advances you have received (including any used to finance loan costs or purchase an annuity) plus interest. In some plans, your debt equals a fixed percentage of your home's value

But your debt is limited by the loan's non-recourse feature. And that generally equals the net proceeds from the sale of your home. In some plans, the non-recourse limit is a fixed percentage of your home's value.

No matter how the loan is structured, the formula for leftover equity is simple:

☐ If the net proceeds from the sale of your home are greater than your debt, you (or your heirs) get the difference in a lump sum of cash.

- For example, if your net sale proceeds are $100,000 and your debt has grown to be $80,000, then your leftover equity would be $20,000.

☐ But if your rising debt has caught up to your loan's non-recourse limit, there is no equity left.

- For example, if your net sale proceeds are $100,000 and your debt has grown to be $100,000, then there is no leftover equity.

Leftover Projections

You can estimate *how much* equity would be left by making assumptions about how long your loan will run, and how fast your home's value will grow.

Leftover equity projections show you important differences between different plans. In particular, they show *how fast* your debt grows (and your equity falls).

Lenders typically provide these types of projections. Just remember that if you want to compare one loan's projections to another's, you must make certain that all the assumptions are the same.

Leftover versus Leftover

For example, a loan with a growing creditline may at some point have a net available creditline that is greater than the amount of equity that would be left if you paid back the loan at that time. In other words, you would end up with more cash if you took out all your remaining creditline just before selling.

If one projection assumes you make the final draw, and another does not, the amounts of leftover cash would be different. *All the leftover equity projections in this book assume that creditlines are drawn down to zero just before the loan is repaid.*

In **Part TWO** you will see leftover equity projections for each reverse mortgage program. In **Part THREE** you will see how these projections compare with each other.

Leftover Planning

There are three basic ways of planning for the type and amount of leftover cash at the end of your loan:

✓ Take out a reverse annuity mortgage that provides monthly advances for life.

✓ Put some or all of your loan funds into a creditline. Whatever you don't use will be there for you to take out just before you sell and move.

✓ Select a plan that limits your debt to some percentage of your home's future value. This preserves the remaining percentage (less selling costs) for you or your heirs.

The annuity approach gives you the security of lifetime income. But the net value of the annuity at the end of your loan may be less than the leftover equity from a plan without an annuity. And you may need a lump sum more than monthly advances at that time.

The creditline method lets you get at your equity during the loan term. But it can only preserve equity for your heirs if you take it out before your death.

By contrast, the debt limit method generally does not let you get at your equity during the loan. But it does preserve equity for you (if you move) or your estate (upon your death).

Part TWO analyzes the specific leftover planning options offered by each reverse mortgage program. **Part THREE** uses leftover projections to compare these options.

All the leftover equity figures assume that the cost of selling your home will be 7% of its value. If your costs are less, or if your loan is repaid without selling your home, then your leftover equity would be greater than the projections in **Parts TWO** and **THREE**.

Beyond the Basics

Chapters 4-8 introduced you to the three basic questions you need to ask about any reverse mortgage:

✓ What do I get? **(Chapter 4)**

✓ What do I pay? **(Chapters 5-7)**

✓ What's left over? **(Chapter 8)**

The next chapter discusses other, program-specific factors that can affect a reverse mortgage's benefits, cost, and leftover cash.

Chapter 9

Other Key Factors

The financial impact of a reverse mortgage may depend on other key factors that can vary from one program to another. Even if the financial features of two programs are identical, the real benefits and risks may not be the same.

For example, as discussed in **Chapter 4**, the net cash you realize from a reverse *annuity* mortgage depends on your tax bracket or public benefit status.

Three other key factors that may vary from program to program are

✔ how much your home is *worth*,

✔ when your loan must be *repaid*, and

✔ the *security* of your cash advances.

Each of these factors can affect what you get, what you pay, and what's left over.

Appraising Your Home

The appraised value of your home is a major factor in determining

☐ how much money you can get;

☐ the amount of any start-up costs calculated as a percent of your home's value; and

☐ the amount of any "shared appreciation" or "percent of value" charges on your loan.

So you need to pay close attention.

The lender arranges for a professional appraiser to determine the current value of your home. In most cases, you are paying for the appraisal. So look at it carefully before you accept it.

Appraising the Appraisal

If the appraised value does not seem reasonable to you, ask the lender or appraiser to explain it. If you wouldn't sell your home for a lot less than you think it's worth, you shouldn't accept an appraisal that's a lot lower than you think it should be.

If the explanation does not make sense to you, or if the appraisal seems much too low, ask for a second opinion by a different appraiser. Or hire your own. It may be worth the extra cost if it puts you in a much better bargaining position.

Valuing Repairs

In some cases, an appraiser may report to a lender that certain repairs are needed to bring a home into "lendable" condition.

If you disagree, you could seek another opinion from a different appraiser. Or appeal to the lender. One program might even have different standards than another.

But keep in mind that repairs can increase the value of your home. If you complete them before loan closing, this greater value can increase your cash advances.

On the other hand, you could pay for the repairs with a lump sum advance from your reverse mortgage. In this case, however, any added value due to the repairs generally would not affect the appraisal.

Payback Time

The real cost of a reverse mortgage depends largely on how long it lasts relative to your life expectancy.

Ordinarily, "how long it lasts" depends on how long you live in your home. But what exactly does that mean? And are there any other conditions that could make your loan due and payable?

The answers to these questions are terribly important. And they can vary from one program to another.

So be certain that you understand the specific meaning of all the conditions that could legally require you to repay your loan. If you don't, you could end up having to sell your home and move long before you would have otherwise decided to do so.

A "Permanent" Move?

All reverse mortgages become due

◆ upon the death of the last surviving borrower,

◆ when you sell your home, or

◆ when you permanently move away.

But the precise meaning of a "permanent" move is not the same in all programs. Most permit you to be away from your home for any purpose for a certain period specified in the loan documents.

But then they may require that the lender approve in writing any longer absence from the home. Or they may require that you arrange for someone to look after the property while you are gone.

Typically, there is some absolute limit to the length of any absence. For example, if you do not live in your home for one year, your loan may become due and payable.

You must read this part of your loan agreement very carefully. Make certain you understand your responsibilities in detail.

Due and Payable

Speaking of responsibilities, you continue to be the owner of your home. And if you do not fulfill your obligations as a homeowner, your loan can become due and payable.

Specifically, the lender can require repayment at any time if you

✓ fail to pay your property taxes,

✓ fail to maintain and repair your home, or

✓ fail to keep your home insured.

These are fairly standard "conditions of default" on any mortgage. On a reverse mortgage, however, lenders typically have the option - but not the obligation - to pay these expenses with your loan funds.

If they exercise it, *this option reduces the amount of your monthly advances or creditline.*

But it is only an option if there is enough money available. If you put all your funds into a creditline and then use it all up, for example, there may be no funds left for the lender to use.

Other default conditions could include

✓ your declaration of bankruptcy,

✓ your donation or abandonment of your home,

✓ your perpetration of fraud or misrepresentation, and

✓ eminent domain or condemnation proceedings involving your home.

Your loan also may include "acceleration" clauses that make it due and payable. Generally, they relate to changes that could affect the security of the loan for the lender. For example,

✓ leasing all or part of your home,

✓ adding a new owner to your home's title,

✓ changing the use of your home from residential to commercial or light manufacturing,

✓ taking out new debt against your home.

Again, you must carefully read the loan documents to make certain you understand all the conditions that can cause your loan to become due and payable. If you are considering more than one reverse mortgage program, be sure to compare the following:

◆ the definition of a permanent move,

◆ the conditions of default, and

◆ the acceleration clauses.

Advance Security

You aren't the only party who could default. Lenders and annuity companies have obligations, too. And if they fail to meet them, *they* will be in default. But where would that leave you?

Prevention

Obviously, you never want to get into a situation where your cash advances don't arrive as they are supposed to. You are paying for those advances and you are counting on them.

Even worse, you never want to learn that your lender or annuity company has failed. You may have certain rights or protections if that happens. But you would much rather avoid altogether the time, cost, and anxiety needed to enforce those rights.

That's why you might prefer a federally-insured reverse mortgage. Or why you might prefer to deal with a company with a long history of solid performance and dependable service. Or a large company of significant financial strength.

Reverse *annuity* mortgage lenders should give you at least two life insurance companies to choose between. Ask for the ratings for these companies published by A.M. Best, Moody's, Duff and Phelps, and Standard and Poor's.

These ratings are usually also available in public libraries. Or you can call Moody's directly at (212) 553-0377, or Standard and Poor's at (212) 208-1527.

Protection

No matter who you deal with, however, you must read the contracts closely to make sure you understand the following:

✓ when a cash advance is considered late;

✓ what you must do to report the late advance;

✓ when late advances turn into default;

✓ what you must do in case of default; and

✓ most important of all, the penalties the lender must pay for late advances and for default.

Penalties

The stronger the penalties on the lender, the less likely you are to face late advances or outright default. The best protection is a penalty so strong that it would not make financial sense for a lender to be late or to default.

In one program, late loan advances trigger a 10% penalty. In another, the lender loses current interest while advances are late. And in another plan, the default penalty is that the lender loses *all* interest on the loan.

You have to be careful in evaluating contractual penalties, however. For example,

☐ If your home's value declines to a point where it is less than the total of your loan advances, then "the loss of all interest" is no penalty at all.

If a lender isn't *owed* any interest (because the principal alone exceeds the non-recourse limit), then the lender can't *lose* any.

☐ If your rising loan balance catches up with the value of your home, then "the loss of current interest" is no penalty at all.

If a lender can no longer *charge* current interest (because the loan balance has already reached the non-recourse limit), then the lender can't *lose* any.

In either of these situations it could be financially advantageous for a lender to default. There would be no real contractual penalty for discontinuing cash advances as promised.

If, on the other hand, the "lost" interest must be contractually *subtracted* from the amount you owe, then it would be more than a phantom penalty.

These might seem like unlikely possibilities. But if they do happen, they are most likely to occur late in the life of a loan - when you may be least inclined or able to deal with it.

In any case, the best time to safeguard your future rights is before you take out a reverse mortgage. Comb the loan documents carefully, and question any provisions that appear to jeopardize your security.

What's Next

Congratulations! You've completed **Part ONE**. You now know what a reverse mortgage is. And what to look for when you see one.

Take a break if you like. You've taken in a lot. So you might want to let it digest a bit before pushing on.

When you're ready to dive back in, I'll meet you in **Part TWO**. There you'll see all kinds of reverse mortgages, and look them over one by one. That will prepare you for **Part THREE**, when you'll size them up side by side, and in relation to your specific needs.

Part

TWO

Nest Egg
Choices

Chapter 10

Previewing the Choices

Which reverse mortgage - if any - is best for you? Before you can answer that question, you need to understand

◆ what the different types of reverse mortgages can do for you;

◆ how much they really cost; and

◆ how much equity they would leave you or your heirs when the loan is repaid.

Part TWO answer these questions.

Surprising Differences

Before learning otherwise, most people assume that all reverse mortgage programs are pretty much the same. A few small differences in interest rates, fees, or cash advances, perhaps. But basically similar in overall design.

Nothing could be further from the truth!

Although all reverse mortgages share certain common features, there are major differences in the basic structure of the various programs. As you learn about them in detail, you probably will be surprised at how fundamentally different they can be.

Different Benefits

In **Part ONE**, you learned in general that different programs offer different types and combinations of cash advances. In **Part TWO**, you will see in detail that one program might meet your cash needs exactly while another might not come anywhere close.

Table 5 gives you a sneak preview of the types of cash advances provided by certain programs. Even a quick peek shows you that no two programs provide the same array of choices.

None of them lets you commit all your available funds to any of the different types of cash advances. And none of the advance types is available in every plan. **Part TWO** also will show you how the cash advance *amounts* differ from one program to another.

Table 5: Cash Advance Choices for Selected Reverse Mortgage Programs

REVERSE MORTGAGE PLANS	Can you take all available funds as			monthly advances for	
	a single lump sum of cash?	a creditline that you control?	a fixed term of years?	as long as you live in your home?	the rest of your life?
HUD/HECM	yes	yes	yes	yes	no
Household	yes	yes	no	no	no
HomeFirst	yes	yes	no	no	yes
Freedom	yes	no	yes	no	yes
Fixed-Term	no	no	yes	no	no
Public Sector*	yes*	no	yes*	no	no

* **Public Sector** plans provide EITHER a one-time advance for home repairs only OR annual advances for property tax payment only OR monthly advances for a fixed period of time.

Different Costs

In **Part ONE**, you learned in general that different programs charge different types of loan costs. In **Part TWO**, you will see in detail that the real, total cost of many of these programs ranges from

 ◆ more than you ever imagined, to

 ◆ less than you ever imagined.

Table 6 gives you a sneak preview of the types of *itemized* loan costs charged by selected programs. This checklist is not easy to follow - even for financial professionals.

But that's just the point. It shows you the futility of trying to compare the total cost of different reverse mortgage programs using itemized costs only.

Part TWO does explain the itemized costs of each program. But it also presents TLC tables that reveal the total cost of these programs on an annual average basis. Later, **Part THREE** will show you how the TLC rates of different programs compare.

Sorting the Programs

Part TWO looks at the various reverse mortgage programs one at a time. **Chapters 11-18** are grouped according to three broad categories relating to use and availability.

Table 6: Major Costs* of Selected Reverse Mortgage Programs

	FEES	INTEREST	OTHER
HUD/ HECM	origination fee varies by local lender; up to $1,800 may be financed	1-year Treasury + 1.6% adjusted yearly; 2% annual & 5% overall caps	insurance = 2% of value (subject to limits) + .5% added to periodic rate
Household	origination: 2.0% of value at closing (minimum is $2,000; max. is $5,000)	prime + 3% adjusted monthly, no cap; overall min. 8%, max. 21%	
HomeFirst (costs for lifetime advances only)	origination: 1.5% of value at closing (min. $2,000); maturity fee = 2.0% of value at loan maturity	9.75% fixed rate on lump sum & monthly advances; 12.5% fixed rate on creditline advances	required purchase of annuity (e.g., $10,660 for single aged 75); up to 50% of home appreciation during loan term
Freedom	(if borrower selects maximum benefits) total amount owed at end of loan equals home value *at that time* minus 7% of appreciation since closing times 75% **OR** - if it is greater - 75% of value *at closing* reduced by 3.75% for each year of borrower's life expectancy at closing; **BUT**, if loan is repaid within 4 years, total amount owed equals the devalued 75% plus 13% interest compounded annually over the life of the loan		

* *Table does not include application fees or third-party closing costs.*

93

Chapters 11-14 look at the multi-purpose plans that were being offered as this book went to press late in 1994:

☐ the HUD/HECM plan **(Chapter 11)**,

☐ the Household plan **(Chapter 12)**,

☐ the HomeFirst plan **(Chapter 13)**, and

☐ the Freedom plan **(Chapter 14)**.

Chapters 15 and **16** preview multi-purpose plans that are expected to become available during 1995:

☐ the Fannie Mae plan **(Chapter 15)**, and

☐ the Republic plan **(Chapter 16)**.

Chapters 17 and **18** analyze plans with more limited cash benefits that are best suited for specialized needs and circumstances:

☐ fixed-term plans **(Chapter 17)**, and

☐ public sector plans **(Chapter 18)**.

Fixed-term plans are the only reverse mortgages that do not safeguard your right to remain in your home for as long as you choose. Most *public sector plans* must be used for specific purposes like making home repairs or paying property taxes.

A Dynamic Market

Chapters 11-18 are based on information provided by lenders in the Fall of 1994. But the reverse mortgage market is young and dynamic.

Specific details of each plan may change from time to time. New benefits may be added, and costs may change. Plan features may even vary from one state to another. Over time, new plans will become available and some current plans may be discontinued.

But the range of programs analyzed in **Part TWO** is quite broad. So the analysis introduces you to a wide array of reverse mortgage options. It shows you how to break down these plans into their basic elements. And that will equip you to take on any new wrinkles that come down the pike.

Finding Reverse Mortgages

Not all plans are available in all areas. **Appendix B** gives you the details on which plans were available in which areas in November of 1994.

You can get a current list of all reverse mortgage lenders from the National Center for Home Equity Conversion.* Its frequently updated "Reverse Mortgage Locator" shows you how to locate the plans available in your state.

---

* Send a self-addressed, stamped, business-size envelope and $1.00 to "NCHEC Locator, 7373 147th St. W., Apple Valley MN 55124."

Since most plans are relatively new, they haven't yet become widely available. Only the federally-insured "HUD/HECM" program was available on a broad national basis by late 1994.

But the newer plans were about to be offered through lenders in the federal program. So prospects for greater availability were excellent in most states - except Texas.*

Off We Go

The time has now come to put aside the general and get into the specific. So take a deep breath and turn with me now to **Chapter 11** for a closer look at the first plan on our list: the federally-insured "HUD/ HECM" program.

---

*Texas is the only state with a serious legal barrier to most reverse mortgages - and many other types of home equity lending. The Texas constitution permits loans against home equity only if they are restricted to purchasing, repairing, or paying property taxes on homes. Since most reverse mortgages can be used for other purposes, they - along with conventional home equity loans - have not been offered in Texas. The only reverse mortgages available there have been nonprofit or public sector loans for home repairs and property tax payments.

On April 29, 1994, the U.S. Court of Appeals, Fifth Circuit (First Gibraltar v. Morales; case # 93-8170) found that reverse mortgages could be offered in Texas based on a 1982 federal law pre-empting the Texas constitution. By late 1994, however, the State of Texas was appealing the decision, and House Banking Chairman Henry Gonzales (D-Tex) had secured passage of federal legislation to over-ride the federal pre-emption. It is possible that this could be overturned in the next Congress, however. So stay tuned.

Chapter 11

The HUD/HECM Plan

You can call it the HUD plan. You can call it the HECM plan. You can even call it the FHA plan. But whatever you call it, it's the only reverse mortgage insured by the federal government.

"HUD" is the U. S. Department of Housing and Urban Development, the federal agency that insures HECM loans. "HECM" stands for Home Equity Conversion Mortgage, the name of the HUD program that issues the insurance. "FHA" is the Federal Housing Administration, the part of HUD that handles the HECM program.

Where and Who

The HUD plan is the most widely available reverse mortgage program. By late 1994, you could find it in 47 states. **Appendix B** identifies lenders offering the program at that time.

To qualify for a HECM loan,

✓ you - and any other owners of your home - must be aged 62 or over;

✓ at least one owner must live in your home as a principal residence;

✓ your home must be a single-family dwelling or part of a HUD-approved condominium or planned unit development (PUD);

✓ your home must meet HUD's minimum property standards, which generally means it must not violate any building codes; and

✓ you must attend an information session on reverse mortgages by a HUD-approved counseling agency.

HUD-HECM lenders will refer you to approved counseling agencies. Lenders and counselors help you figure out if you qualify for the program. They know how to deal with special situations. And they have the latest information on any changes in program rules.

For example, in 1995 the Congress will consider a proposal to expand the program to include duplexes, triplexes, and 4-unit properties. HUD counselors and lenders will be the first to know about any changes.

HUD-HECM Benefits

The HECM plan provides a wide array of cash advance choices. You can take all of your loan as

☐ a single lump sum of cash, or as

☐ a creditline that grows over time, or as

☐ a monthly cash advance for a fixed period, or for as long as you live in your home.

In addition, you can

☐ choose any combination of these options, and

☐ change your cash advance choices at any time in the future.

Figuring How Much

The amount of money you can get from the HECM program depends primarily on three factors: your age, the "expected" interest rate on your loan, and the value of your home.

Appendix C spells out exactly how these factors are used to determine the amount of money you can get. But even if you're not interested in the details, you need to know a little more about these factors.

Age and Interest

If there is more than one owner of the property, the age of the *youngest* borrower is used to figure out your cash advance amounts.

The "expected" interest rate is different from the rate initially charged on most HECM loans. The expected rate is tied to the U. S. Treasury Securities 10-year rate, which is published each week. HECM lenders can tell you what it is at any given time.

"203-b" Limits on Home Value

The appraised value of your home is used to find how much money you can get from a HECM loan. But this value is subject to certain limits that vary from one area to another.

They are called "203-b limits" because that is the section of the National Housing Act that defines them. Based on recent stautory changes, they range from $77,197 to $152,362.50 in the continental U. S. (The latter figure will be "rounded up" to $152,363 for the analyses in this book, although it may be "rounded down" to $152,362 when published by HUD.)

If your home is worth more than the 203-b limit in your area, you are still eligible for a HECM loan - but the amount of money you can get will be based on the 203-b limit, not on your home's actual value.

100

For example, if your home is valued at $125,000 and the 203-b limit in your area is $100,000, then your cash advances are the same as they would be if your home were valued at $100,000.

The 203-b limits are subject to change every year. HECM lenders (see **Appendix B**) and counselors can tell you what the current limit is in your area.

Analyzing How Much

The amount of money you can get from a HECM loan also depends on how you want it paid to you: lump sum, creditline, monthly advance, or some combination of these three types of cash advances.

Lump Sums & Creditlines

Table 7 shows how much you could get if you take it all as a single lump sum of cash or as a creditline.

☐ if the value of your home ÷ or the 203-b limit in your area, whichever is less - equals $50,000, $100,000, or $150,000;

☐ if the expected interest rate on the loan is 8%, 9%, or 10%;

☐ if the age of the youngest borrower at time of closing is 65, 70, 75, 80, 85, or 90; and

☐ if your financed loan costs equal those assumed in **Table 7** (see note at bottom of page 103).

101

Table 7: HUD-HECM Lump Sum or Creditline at Various
Home Values, Ages, and Interest Rates*

HOME VALUE	AGE	Lump Sum or Creditline* When Expected Interest Rate Is		
		8%	9%	10%
$50,000	65	$13,079	$9,933	$7,392
	70	16,276	13,203	10,543
	75	19,923	16,916	14,329
	80	23,849	21,147	18,674
	85	27,943	25,587	23,369
	90	32,019	30,103	28,231
$100,000	65	$31,929	$25,333	$19,992
	70	38,226	31,803	26,243
	75	45,373	39,116	33,729
	80	52,999	47,397	42,274
	85	60,843	55,987	51,419
	90	68,469	64,553	60,731
$150,000	65	$50,779	$40,733	$32,592
	70	60,176	50,403	41,943
	75	70,823	61,316	53,129
	80	82,149	73,647	68,874
	85	93,743	86,387	79,469
	90	104,919	99,003	93,231

* See note at bottom of next page on loan cost assumptions.

The amounts in **Table 7*** can be divided between a lump sum and a creditline. For example, a 75-year-old borrower living in a $100,000 home getting a HECM loan at 9% expected interest could select

☐ a lump sum or creditline of $39,116; or

☐ any *combination* of lump sum and creditline that totals $39,116, for example, a lump sum of $10,000 and a creditline of $29,116.

Creditline Growth

If you select a creditline, it will increase by the loan's expected rate plus 0.5%. In the example above, a $39,116 creditline would increase at 9.5% (.7917 per month) to become $42,998 after one year, $47,265 after two years, and so on.

The amount of money left in your creditline at any time (the "net" amount) equals whatever the creditline has grown to become (the "gross" amount) MINUS all the money you have taken out and the interest that has been charged on that money.

After each creditline advance, the lender sends you a statement showing how much money is left in your creditline. HUD is currently developing new policies that would lead to more frequent statements.

---

*Tables 7-12 assume that you finance all loan costs, including an origination fee of $1,800, a monthly servicing fee of $25, the mortgage insurance premium, and closing costs that total $1,000 on a $50,000 home, $1,400 on a $100,000 home, and $1,800 on a $150,000 home. If your costs are less, your advances will be greater - and vice versa.

Plus a Monthly Advance

You can combine a lump sum, a creditline, or both with a monthly advance. A monthly advance does not increase or decrease in dollar amount over time. It can be paid to you

- ◆ for a specific number of years that you select (a "term" plan) or

- ◆ for as long as you live in your home (a "tenure" plan).

You can combine these different types of advances in any way you want. **Table 8** shows some of the combinations that could be selected by a 75-year-old borrower living in a $150,000 home with a loan at 9% expected interest.

For example, if this borrower selected a lump sum of $10,000 and a creditline of $20,000, she also could get any of the following: a monthly advance of $271 for as long as she lives in her home, $324 each month for 15 years, $402 each month for 10 years, or $653 each month for 5 years.

Table 8 makes two things clear:

- ☐ If you put more money into a lump sum or creditline, the monthly advances are less.

- ☐ If you select a shorter term of monthly advances, the amount of the advance is greater.

Table 8: HUD-HECM Monthly Advances Combined with Lump Sums and Creditlines for a 75-Year-Old Borrower Living in a $150,000 Home*

	+ Monthly Advance For			
	Tenure	15 Years	10 Years	5 Years
Any combination of a lump sum and creditline totaling . . .				
0	$532	$635	$787	$1,278
$10,000	445	532	659	1,069
20,000	358	428	530	861
30,000	271	324	402	653
40,000	185	221	274	444
50,000	98	117	145	236
61,316	0	0	0	0

*See note at bottom of page 103 and text on page 104.

Monthly Advances Only

Table 8 shows that you get the largest possible monthly advance if you do not take a lump sum or a creditline. **Tables 9** and **10** provide the details.

Table 9 shows how much you could get on a *tenure* plan, that is, a monthly advance for as long as you live in your home. **Table 10** shows how much you could get on a *term* plan - monthly advances for a fixed period of time. Both tables assume that you take no lump sum and no creditline.

*Table 9: HUD-HECM Monthly **Tenure** Advance* Only at
Various Home Values, Ages, and Interest Rates*

		Monthly Tenure Advance* When Expected Interest Rate Is		
		8%	9%	10%
HOME VALUE	AGE			
$50,000	65	$97	$81	$66
	70	124	110	96
	75	159	147	134
	80	206	196	185
	85	273	265	256
	90	394	386	378
$100,000	65	$237	$207	$178
	70	292	265	238
	75	363	339	316
	80	457	438	418
	85	595	580	563
	90	843	829	812
$150,000	65	$377	$332	$290
	70	459	420	380
	75	566	532	497
	80	708	681	652
	85	917	895	871
	90	1,292	1,271	1,247

*See note at bottom of page 103.

Table 10: HUD-HECM Monthly Term Advances* Only at Various Home Values, Ages, and 9% Interest

HOME VALUE	AGE	Monthly Term Advance* For		
		5 years	10 years	15 years
$50,000	65	$207	$128	$103
	70	275	170	137
	75	352	217	175
	80	441	271	219
	85	533	328	265**
	90	627	386**	386**
$100,000	65	$528	$325	$262
	70	663	408	329
	75	815	502	405
	80	988	608	491
	85	1,167	719	580**
	90	1,345	829**	829**
$150,000	65	$849	$523	$422
	70	1,050	647	522
	75	1,278	787	635
	80	1,535	945	763
	85	1,800	1,109	895**
	90	2,063	1,271**	1,271**

*See note at bottom of page 103. **The tenure advance is shown because it is greater than the term advance.

HUD-HECM Costs

Back in **Chapter 5,** you learned there are two ways
of evaluating reverse mortgage costs:

☐ the itemized approach that looks at
   each cost item one at a time; and

☐ the Total Loan Cost (TLC) method that
   shows the total annual average cost.

First let's look at the itemized checklist of HECM
costs. Then we'll consider the pattern of TLC rates on
typical HECM loans.

Itemized Costs

The HECM checklist includes five cost categories:
origination fee, closing costs, mortgage insurance,
servicing fee, and interest rates.

Origination Fee

An origination fee pays the lender for preparing
your paperwork and processing your loan, that is, for
"originating" your loan. This fee can vary from lender
to lender. Often it is the only cost that differs from
one HECM lender to another. So be sure to shop
around.

You can finance (that is, use the HECM loan to pay
for) up to $1,800 of the origination fee. If the fee is
greater, you must pay the difference in cash.

Closing Costs

Closing any mortgage requires a variety of third-party services such as an appraisal, title search and insurance, surveys, inspections, recording fees, mortgage taxes, credit checks, and others.

Closing costs on a HECM loan vary somewhat with the value of the home. They also can vary a lot from one state or area to another. But all the HECM lenders in a given area are likely to charge about the same closing costs on any specific loan.

Generally, these costs range from about $1,000 to $1,800, although in some states they may be over $3,000 - especially on higher-valued homes. High state mortgage taxes are often to blame.

You can generally finance all closing costs with the loan. A lender may require a cash application fee to pay for an appraisal or credit check. But you can get it back by adding it to your loan balance at closing - if you decide to go through with the loan.

Mortgage Insurance

The cost of the HECM insurance premium also can be financed. It is charged in two parts:

✓ 2% of your home's value (or 2% of the 203-b limit in your area, whichever is less) is charged at closing; and

✓ 0.5% is added to the interest rate charged on your rising loan balance.

Servicing Fee

On a HECM loan, servicing includes making loan advances, transferring insurance premiums to HUD, sending regular account statements, paying property taxes and insurance from the loan at your request, and monitoring your compliance with your obligations under the loan agreement.

The servicing fee is generally a fixed dollar amount that is added to your loan balance each month. Typical servicing fees range from $20 to $30.

Interest Rates

Almost all HECM lenders charge an annually adjustable rate of interest on their HECM loans. This means that the interest rate can change once each year. But by federal regulation any change in the rate

- ◆ must be the same change (increase or decrease) that occurred during the previous year in the U.S. Treasury Securities one-year rate

- ◆ subject to a limit or "cap" of two percentage points per year and five total percentage points over the life of the loan.

A few lenders offer a lower rate that may be adjusted every month. Changes in this rate also must be tied to the one-year Treasury rate. But the only limit is a 10 percentage point cap over the life of the loan.

The advantages of this rate are that

✓ a lower beginning rate means a lower expected rate, which means larger loan advances; and

✓ the monthly adjustable rate will be lower than the annually adjustable rate as long as changes in the Treasury rate are less than two points per year and five points over the life of the loan.

Once the loan begins, however, changes in an adjustable interest rate do not affect your loan advances. You continue to get the same monthly advances and your gross creditline continues to grow at the loan's expected rate plus 0.5%.

What does change is the rate at which your loan balance grows. This affects how much is left in your net creditline, and how much equity is left at the end of your loan.

Total Loan Costs

Table 11 projects Total Loan Cost rates on a HECM loan to a 75-year-old living in a $150,000 home at 8.81% expected interest. The table shows TLC rates for three cash advance options:

◆ a single lump sum of $63,672 at closing;

◆ a creditline of $63,672 - assuming half is taken at closing, and none after that; and

◆ a monthly tenure advance of $544.

111

Part TWO: Nest Egg Choices

Table 11: TLC Rates on a HECM Loan to a 75-Year-Old Borrower Living in a $150,000 Home*

	At End of Year	TLC when annual average home appreciation equals		
		0%	3%	6%
LUMP SUM	2	14.7%	14.7%	14.7%
	7	11	11	11
	12	6.6	9.5	10.4
	17	4.6	7.6	10.1
	22	3.6	6.5	9.4
CREDIT-LINE	2	19.6%	19.6%	19.6%
	7	12.6	12.6	12.6
	12	11.4	11.4	11.4
	17	8.7	10.8	10.8
	22	6.7	9.7	10.5
MONTHLY TENURE	2	51.5%	51.5%	51.5%
	7	14.7	14.7	14.7
	12	8.8	11.7	11.7
	17	2.6	7.8	10.7
	22	-0.3	5.2	9.7

*See note at bottom of page 103 and text on page 111. Expected rate used in this table (8.81%) was the expected rate for 9/1/94.

112

As discussed in **Chapter 6**, TLCs vary with the type of cash advance selected, the length of the loan, and the rate at which a home's value grows. As you can see in **Table 11**, TLCs are generally lowest on lump sum advances and greatest on monthly advances.

TLCs on creditlines depend on how the creditline is used. The assumption in **Table 11** is that you use half of it ($31,836) at closing, and none after that.

If you were to take more of the creditline at closing, the TLC would look more like lump sum TLCs. On the other hand, if you used the creditline more like a monthly advance or some other type of regular, periodic advance, then the TLC rates would look more like the TLCs on monthly tenure advances.

No matter which type of advance you select, however, TLC rates are lowest

✓ when you live in your home the longest, and

✓ when your home's value grows the least.

HUD-HECM Leftovers

Table 12 shows how much cash would be left if a typical HECM loan ended at various points in the future. It is based on the same assumptions used to make **Table 11**, and it shows leftover equity from the same lump sum, creditline, and monthly advances as in **Table 11**.

Table 12: Leftover Equity on a HECM Loan to a 75-Year-
Old Borrower Living in a $150,000 Home*

| | At End of Year | Leftover equity when annual average appreciation equals | | |
		0%	3%	6%
LUMP SUM	2	$54,245	$62,741	$71,487
	7	2,032	34,099	72,288
	12	0	0	60,218
	17	0	0	23,169
	22	0	0	0
CREDIT-LINE*	2	$92,569	$101,065	$109,811
	7	62,966	95,033	133,222
	12	96,881*	96,881*	157,100
	17	154,037*	154,037*	177,206
	22	244,911*	244,911*	244,911*
MONTHLY TENURE	2	$116,500	$124,996	$133,742
	7	59,352	91,419	129,608
	12	0	27,882	109,689
	17	0	0	60,161
	22	0	0	0

*Leftover equity equals home value minus total amount owed minus the cost of selling the home, which is assumed to be 7% of the home's value. Leftover equity also includes remaining creditline assumed to be withdrawn just prior to loan maturity.

Table 12 reveals three general patterns about the amount of leftover equity.

Appreciation

The first pattern is that greater appreciation rates produce greater leftover equity. Makes sense: the more your home is worth,

◆ the more equity will be left after paying off the loan, and

◆ the less likely your rising loan balance will catch up to your home's value, leaving no remaining equity.

Time

The second general pattern is that leftover equity decreases over time. This general pattern can be seen in **Table 12** on lump sum and tenure advances.

On the creditline advance, however, the falling equity pattern does not hold. It doesn't because the table assumes you withdraw the remaining creditline just prior to loan maturity. And in the HECM program, the creditline grows over time.

If you were to die before you could withdraw the remaining creditline, then the amount of leftover equity to your heirs would be much less than the amounts marked with an asterisk (*) in the creditline section of the table.

115

Advance Types

The third pattern is that remaining equity depends on the type of cash advance selected. It is lowest for the lump sum borrower who takes all the money available to her at closing ($63,672).

On the other hand, it is generally greatest for the creditline borrower who takes half that amount at closing, and then nothing more until just before loan maturity. The creditline borrower has the greatest control over the amount of leftover equity.

✓ If she takes nearly all her creditline at closing, her leftover equity will resemble the lump sum borrower's.

✓ If she takes advances on a regular, periodic basis, her leftover equity will resemble the tenure borrower's.

✓ If she uses her creditline very little, her leftover equity will be greater than the amounts shown in **Table 12**.

Other HUD-HECM Features

So far you have seen the three main financial elements of a HECM loan: cash benefits, itemized and total costs, and leftover equity. Now you need to look at three key questions that go beyond these financial matters:

✔ What happens if you don't get HECM cash advances on time?

✔ What happens if a HECM lender fails?

✔ When exactly must you repay a HECM loan?

Late Advances

Monthly loan advances must be sent to you by the first business day of each month. Creditline advances must be sent to you within five business days of your written request.

If a loan advance is late, the lender must pay you a late charge equal to 10% of the advance amount. For each additional day the payment is late, the lender must pay you interest on the late advance. The total late charge may not exceed $500.

Lender Default

Because it is the only federally-insured reverse mortgage, the HECM plan is the most secure reverse mortgage you will find. The federal government stands behind and guaranties all HECM loans.

This means that if a lender goes bankrupt or is otherwise incapable of making advances as promised, the U.S. Department of Housing and Urban Development (HUD) will step in and take over the lender's obligations.

117

The papers you sign at closing establish your relationship with your originating lender *and* with the federal government. (That's why there are so many papers to sign!)

This gives you the strongest possible protection against lender default. If your lender fails, you won't have to go to court to get your money.

Repayment

As with most reverse mortgages, you must repay a HECM loan in full when the last surviving borrower dies or sells the home. In addition, the loan may become due and payable with HUD approval if

✓ the property falls into disrepair and you fail to correct the problem; or

✓ all borrowers permanently move to a new principal residence; or

✓ due to physical or mental illness, the last surviving borrower fails to live in the home as a principal residence for 12 months in a row; or

✓ you fail to pay your property taxes or hazard insurance premiums, or violate any other borrower obligation.

In these cases, you will be referred to HUD counselors before any other action is taken.

HUD-HECM Summary

The HUD-HECM program

✓ is available in 47 states (see **Appendix B**);

✓ offers a broad array of cash advance options at closing plus the ability to change your cash advance choices at any time;

✓ is the most secure reverse mortgage plan; and

✓ limits the amount of equity you can convert into cash through its "203-b" limits, which are based on median home values in each area.

Chapter 12

The Household Plan

In June of 1994, Household Senior Services (HSS) unveiled the first privately-sponsored creditline reverse mortgage.

HSS is a division of Household Bank, which is part of Household International - a consumer finance corporation established in 1878. With current assets of $32 billion, Household International is one of the largest financial services companies in the United States.

Household's creditline plan is a very simple reverse mortgage that is very easy to understand.

Where and Who

By late 1994, the Household plan was being offered in Florida, Georgia, Illinois, Kentucky, Maryland, Michigan, Ohio, and Virginia. During 1995, the plan is expected to become available in California and other major states. To qualify for a Household loan,

✓ you - and any other owners of your home - must be aged 62 or over;

✓ at least one owner must live in your home as a principal residence;

✓ your home must be a single-family dwelling or an approved condominium; and

✓ you must have enough equity to qualify for a lump sum or creditline of at least $10,000.

Household Benefits

The Household plan lets you take all the money available to you as

☐ a single lump sum of cash, or as

☐ a creditline, or as

☐ a lump sum and a creditline.

How It Works

Household's creditline is easy to use. You just write a check, using a special creditline checkbook. The amount of each check is subtracted from your available creditline and added to your loan balance.

No repayment is required for as long as you live in your home. But if you want, you can pay back any amount at any time. The amount of remaining credit equals the original creditline **minus** all the checks you have written **plus** any repayments you have made.

How Much You Get

The amount of the lump sum or creditline depends on your age, the value of your home, the interest rate at time of loan application, and the amount of any financed loan costs. In no case, however, may the amount be greater than $250,000.

Tables 13-14 show how much money you could get

☐ if the value of your home equals $150,000, $200,000, or $250,000;

☐ if the initial interest rate 10%, 11%, or 12%;

☐ if you are a single or joint borrower aged 65, 70, 75, 80, 85, or 90; and

☐ if your financed loan costs equal those described in the note at the bottom of page 126.

*Table 13: Household Benefits for Single Borrowers at
Various Home Values, Ages, and Interest Rates**

HOME VALUE	AGE	Lump Sum or Creditline When Initial Interest Rate Is		
		10%	11%	12%
$150,000	65	$30,000	$25,300	$21,200
	70	36,900	31,900	27,600
	75	49,900	44,800	40,200
	80	60,700	55,800	51,300
	85	81,100	77,000	73,100
	90	94,400	91,600	88,800
$200,000	65	$40,200	$33,900	$28,400
	70	49,400	42,800	36,900
	75	66,700	59,900	53,800
	80	81,100	74,600	68,500
	85	108,300	102,900	97,700
	90	126,100	122,300	118,600
$250,000	65	$50,400	$42,500	$35,700
	70	61,900	53,600	46,300
	75	83,500	75,100	67,400
	80	101,600	93,400	85,800
	85	135,600	128,800	122,300
	90	157,800	153,000	148,400

* See note at bottom of page 126 on loan cost assumptions.

*Table 14: Household Benefits for **Joint Borrowers** at Various Home Values, Ages, and Interest Rates**

HOME VALUE	AGE	Lump Sum or Creditline When Initial Interest Rate Is		
		10%	11%	12%
$150,000	65	$24,200	$19,800	$16,100
	70	30,000	25,300	21,200
	75	40,800	35,800	31,300
	80	49,900	44,800	40,200
	85	66,900	62,200	57,800
	90	81,100	77,000	73,100
$200,000	65	$32,500	$26,600	$21,600
	70	40,200	33,900	28,400
	75	54,600	47,900	42,000
	80	66,700	59,900	53,800
	85	89,400	83,100	77,200
	90	108,300	102,900	97,700
$250,000	65	$40,800	$33,400	$27,200
	70	50,400	42,500	35,700
	75	68,400	60,100	52,600
	80	83,500	75,100	67,400
	85	111,900	104,000	96,700
	90	135,600	128,800	122,300

* See note at bottom of page 126 on loan cost assumptions.

Lump + Line

The amounts* in **Tables 13** and **14** can be divided between a lump sum and a creditline. For example, an 80-year-old single borrower living in a $200,000 home with an initial loan rate of 11% could select

♦ a lump sum or creditline of $74,600; or

♦ any *combination* of lump sum and creditline that totals $74,600, for example, a lump sum of $14,600 and a creditline of $60,000.

Larger Home Values

If your home is worth more than $250,000, you can use **Tables 13-14** to estimate the cash amounts available to you.

For example, if your home is worth $300,000, simply double the amount for a $150,000 home. Or, if your home's value is $350,000, just add the amounts for a $150,000 home and a $200,000 home.

The result probably will be a little less than you can actually get. But it will give you a fairly close estimate. Just remember that in no case does Household offer creditlines greater than $250,000.

---

*Tables 13-14 assume that you finance all loan costs, including an origination fee that equals 2% of your home's value and closing costs that total $1,800 on a $150,000 home, $2,200 on a $200,000 home, and $2,600 on a $250,000 home. If your closing costs are less, then your lump sum or creditline would be larger, and vice versa.

126

Monthly Projections

The Household plan does not guarantee monthly advances for as long as you live in your home, or for life.

But if you plan to take monthly advances from a Household creditline, you can easily figure out

✓ how long a given amount would last, or

✓ how much you could take for a given period.

For example, if your creditline is $48,000 and you expect to take $400 per month, you simply divide the creditline by the amount of the monthly advance.

The answer in this case is 120 months - or ten years. That's how long you could get $400 per month.

On the other hand, if you want to know how much money you could get each month for a given period, just divide the creditline by the number of months.

For example, if your creditline is $54,000 and you want monthly advances for 15 years (180 months), then you could take $300 per month.

Household Costs

The cost of the Household plan is relatively easy to understand. It involves fewer types of itemized costs than most plans.

Itemized Costs

The checklist of itemized costs in the Household plan includes an origination fee, closing costs, and interest.

Origination Fee

The cost of originating the plan is generally 2% of your home's value (2.5% in Georgia). The minimum origination fee is $2,000, and the maximum is $5,000.

Closing Costs

Closing costs generally include an appraisal, title search, title insurance, required inspections, and any recording fees or mortgage taxes. A nonrefundable application fee of $100 is credited against these costs.

Interest

The Household plan charges a variable interest rate on the loan balance that equals the "prime rate" plus 3%. The prime rate is subject to change on the first business day of each month, when it is published in the Wall Street Journal.

So the rate charged on this loan may change as often as every month based on changes in the prime rate. In other words, the rate will generally equal the current prime rate plus 3%.

There is no limit or cap on how much the rate may change during any year. But over the life of the loan, the minimum rate is 8% and the maximum rate is 21% or as dictated by law.

No Other Charges

The Household plan does not include a risk-pooling fee, a servicing fee, or any cost based on appreciation.

Total Loan Costs

Table 15 projects Total Loan Cost (TLC) rates on a Household loan to a 75-year-old borrower living in a home worth $150,000.

The table is based on interest rates that are comparable with the rates and consistent with the methods used in the HUD/HECM program for September 1, 1994 (see note at bottom of next page). It assumes that all fees and closing costs (taken from **Table 13**) are financed with the loan.

Table 15 shows TLC rates for

♦ a single lump sum of $46,000 at closing; and

♦ a creditline of $46,000 - assuming half is taken at closing, and none after that.

Household Leftovers

Table 16 shows how much cash would be left if the lump sum and creditline loans in **Table 15** ended at various points in the future. The assumptions in **Table 16** are the same as those in **Table 15** (see the note at the bottom of the next page).

Table 15: TLC Rates on a Household Loan to a
75-Year-Old Borrower in a $150,000 Home*

	At End of Year	TLC when annual average home appreciation equals		
		0%	3%	6%
LUMP SUM	2	17.4%	17.4%	17.4%
	7	13.8	13.8	13.8
	12	9.3	12.3	13.2
	17	6.5	9.5	12.4
	22	5.1	8	10.9
CREDIT-LINE	2	22%	22%	22%
	7	15.1	15.1	15.1
	12	14	14	14
	17	10.7	13.5	13.5
	22	8.2	11.2	13.3

***Table 15** is based on an initial rate of 10.75%, which is 3% more than the prime rate was on 9/1/94. It is unlikely, however, that this initial rate will turn out to be the annual average rate charged on the loan balance. So the TLCs are based on loan balance projections that would be generated by an expected annual average rate of 12.4%.

The difference between the initial and expected rates (1.65%) is the difference between the 1-year and the 10-year Treasury rate for 9/1/94. This is the same method used in the HUD/HECM program to estimate the difference between initial and expected interest rates.

Table 16: Leftover Equity on a Household Loan to a 75-Year-Old Borrower in a $150,000 Home*

	At End of Year	Leftover equity when annual average appreciation equals		
		0%	3%	6%
LUMP SUM	2	$74,485	$82,981	$91,727
	7	19,025	51,092	89,281
	12	0	0	57,458
	17	0	0	0
	22	0	0	0
CREDIT-LINE*	2	$103,921	$112,417	$121,163
	7	73,571	105,638	143,827
	12	23,000*	76,726	158,533
	17	23,000*	23,000*	149,261
	22	23,000*	23,000*	83,204

*See note at bottom of previous page. Leftover equity in this table equals home value minus total amount owed minus the cost of selling the home, which is assumed to be 7% of the home's value. *Leftover equity also includes remaining creditline assumed to be withdrawn just prior to loan maturity.*

Leftover equity varies according to appreciation, time, and advance types. For a discussion of the basic patterns in **Table 16,** see pages 115-116.

Other Household Features

The Household loan generally becomes due and payable when the last surviving borrower dies or sells the home.

Unlike other reverse mortgages, the Household plan places *no limits on temporary absences from the home.* In fact, a *permanent* move is not even listed as a condition that requires repayment.

But the loan may become due and payable if you

✓ fail to pay your property taxes or any special assessments,

✓ fail to maintain your homeowner's insurance,

✓ fail to maintain your home in reasonable condition,

✓ incur a new lien that jeopardizes the lender's security interest, or

✓ perpetrate fraud or misrepresentation in obtaining the loan from Household.

Lender Default

Like other reverse mortgages, the Household plan is subject to state laws on breach of contract, including remedies for the borrower and penalties to the lender.

There aren't any explicit contractual remedies or penalties if the lender fails to advance loan funds as promised.

Household Summary

The Household Senior Services plan

✓ is available in Florida, Georgia, Illinois, Kentucky, Maryland, Michigan, Ohio, and Virginia, and expected in California and other major states during 1995;

✓ offers a simple creditline of up to $250,000 in available credit.

Chapter 13

The HomeFirst Plan

In 1993, Transamerica became the first well-known company to enter the reverse mortgage market.

With over $35 billion in assets, Transamerica is one of the largest financial services companies in the United States. Its pyramid-shaped headquarters is a fixture of the San Francisco skyline.

Transamerica HomeFirst - a subsidiary of the Transamerica Corporation - offered the first reverse mortgage providing monthly cash advances for life. In 1994, the HomeFirst plan was expanded to include new creditline and lump sum options.

Where and Who

By late 1994, the HomeFirst plan was available throughout California, New Jersey, New York, and Pennsylvania. During 1995, the program is expected to expand into other states.

To qualify for a HomeFirst loan,

✓ you must be aged 65 or over;

✓ your home must be worth $100,000 or more;

✓ your home must be a single-family dwelling, duplex, triplex, 4-unit building, condominium, or part of planned unit development (PUD).

HomeFirst Benefits

The HomeFirst plan provides a wide array of cash advance choices. You can take all of your loan as

☐ a single lump sum of cash, or as

☐ a creditline, or as

☐ a monthly cash advance for as long as you live - *no matter where you live.*

You also can select various combinations of these cash advance options.

The amount of money you can get from a Home-First loan depends on a variety of factors, including the type of cash advances you choose.

Creditline or Lump Sum

Table 17 shows how much you could in a single lump sum of cash or a creditline

☐ if the value of your home equals $150,000, $200,000, or $250,000;

☐ if your age is 65, 70, 75, 80, 85, or 90;

☐ if you borrowed in the Fall of 1994 (see below); and

☐ if your financed loan costs equal those described in the note below **Table 17**.

The amounts available to *new* borrowers from HomeFirst are not subject to change when interest rates change each week (as the HUD/HECM advances are) or each month (as the Household advances are).

Instead, HomeFirst establishes a fixed schedule of advances. As long as rates in general do change very much, that schedule remains in force. If and when the overall interest rate environment changes, HomeFirst may adjust its schedule of advances for new borrowers at that time. The advances in **Table 17** were being offered by HomeFirst in November of 1994.

Part TWO: Nest Egg Choices

*Table 17: HomeFirst Benefits - **Lump Sum or Creditline***

HOME VALUE	AGE**	Lump Sum or Creditline
$150,000	65	$19,583
	70	27,788
	75	37,483
	80	48,155
	85	58,392
	90	68,562
$200,000	65	$26,579
	70	37,499
	75	50,400
	80	64,598
	85	78,214
	90	91,738
$250,000	65	$33,576
	70	47,210
	75	63,317
	80	81,040
	85	98,036
	90	114,915

*Available in the Fall of 1994. **Table 17** assumes that you finance all loan costs, including an origination fee equaling 2% of your home's value, and closing costs that total $1,800 on a $150,000 home, $2,200 on a $200,000, and $2,600 on a $250,000 home. If your costs are less, your advances will be greater - and vice versa.
**Age of single borrower or younger age of joint borrowers.

138

Lump + Line

The amounts in **Table 17** can be divided between a lump sum and a creditline. For example, an 80-year-old borrower living in a $200,000 home could select

☐ a lump sum or creditline of $64,598; or

☐ any *combination* of lump sum and creditline that totals $64,598, for example, a lump sum of $10,000 and a creditline of $54,598.

Larger Home Values

If your home is worth more than $250,000 but less than $600,000, you can use **Table 17** to estimate the cash amounts available to you. If your home is worth $300,000, for example, just double the amount for a $150,000 home.

If your home is worth more than $600,000, your lump sum or creditline will equal the amount for a home worth $600,000.

Using the Creditline

Each advance you request must be for a minimum of $500. The amount is subtracted from your available creditline and added to your loan balance.

No repayment is required for as long as you live in your home. But if you want, you can pay back any amount at any time. The amount of remaining credit equals the original creditline **minus** all your advances **plus** any repayments you have made.

Monthly for Life

HomeFirst also offers monthly advances for as long as you live - no matter where you live.

This alternative is actually a separate loan plan, and it offers a limited lump sum or creditline in addition to the monthly advances for life. The costs of this plan are significantly different from the costs of the "stand-alone" creditline or lump sum.

(If you are aged 90 or over, you are not eligible for lifetime monthly advances. But HomeFirst will offer you a fixed-term loan (see **Chapter 17**).

How It Works

First, you receive monthly *loan advances* for a fixed period related to your life expectancy. Then, in the month after the loan advances stop, you start getting monthly *annuity advances* that continue for the rest of your life.

The amount of each annuity advance is the same as each loan advance, with one exception. If you sell and move before the annuity is scheduled to begin, the annuity begins at that time, but at a lower monthly amount than the loan advances.

You may choose between an annuity from Metropolitan Life Insurance (Met Life) or Transamerica Occidental Life Insurance. The monthly advances from Transamerica may be larger. But Met Life is ranked higher by the agencies that rate the financial strength of such companies.

How Much You Get

Table 18 shows the monthly advances available to single and joint borrowers of various ages living in homes of various values. These advances assume that you do not choose to take a creditline or lump sum in addition to your monthly advances.

If you do select an optional creditline or lump sum, this reduces the amount of each monthly advance. The greater the creditline or lump sum, the smaller the monthly advance will be. You must take a monthly advance of at least $150, however, so this limits the amount of your optional creditline or lump sum.

If you take a creditline in addition to your monthly advances, it will increase by 3.5% per year. But it is only available to you until the annuity advances begin.

HomeFirst Costs

The costs of a HomeFirst reverse mortgage depend on which of their plans you choose.

If you select the "standalone" lump sum or creditline (that is, with no monthly advances), the itemized costs are quite simple and straightforward. But if you choose monthly advances for life, the itemized costs are a bit more involved.

In either case, however, the itemized costs can be combined into Total Loan Cost (TLC) rates that simplify the matter considerably.

141

Table 18: HomeFirst Benefits - *Monthly Advances Only*

		single borrower	joint borrowers
HOME VALUE	**AGE**		
$150,000	**65**	$261	$248
	70	369	345
	75	536	486
	80	697	624
	85	941	825
	90	1,337	1,079
$200,000	**65**	$350	$333
	70	494	462
	75	717	651
	80	931	834
	85	1,258	1,103
	90	1,787	1,442
$250,000	**65**	$439	$418
	70	619	579
	75	898	815
	80	1,166	1,044
	85	1,574	1,380
	90	2,236	1,804

*The advances in this table were available in the Fall of 1994. The advances are based on the assumption that you finance all loan costs, including a 2% origination fee, a 2% maturity fee, 50% shared appreciation, and closing costs that total $1,800 on a $150,000 home, $2,200 on a $200,000 home, and $2,600 on a $250,000 home. If your closing costs are less, your advances will be greater - and vice versa.

Itemized Costs

HomeFirst's standalone lump sum or creditline includes the following itemized costs:

- ✓ an origination fee equals 2% of your home's value at closing;

- ✓ closing costs generally include an appraisal, title search, title insurance, required inspections, escrow charges, and any recording fees or mortgage taxes;

- ✓ an annual fee of $100; and

- ✓ an interest rate that equals the U. S. Treasury Securities one-year rate plus 5%, adjustable annually with a lifetime cap 10% greater than the initial rate.

Monthly for Life

If you select HomeFirst's monthly advances for life, the itemized costs are as follows:

- ✓ closing costs (as above);

- ✓ an origination fee equals 1.5% of the home's value or a minimum of $2,000;

- ✓ the cost of an annuity depends on your age (for example, for a 75-year-old single borrower in the Fall of 1994 it was about $10,660);

✓ a 9.75% fixed rate of interest is charged
on the monthly loan advances and optional
lump sum;

✓ 12.5% fixed interest is charged on the
optional creditline advances;

✓ an "appreciation sharing" charge at loan
maturity equals up to 50% of any increase
in home value during the loan term; and

✓ a "maturity fee" equals 2% of the home's
value at loan maturity.

Total Loan Costs

Table 19 projects Total Loan Cost (TLC) rates on
a HomeFirst loan to a 75-year-old borrower living in
a home worth $150,000. It assumes that all fees and
closing costs (taken from **Tables 17** and **18**) are
financed with the loan.*

Table 19 shows TLC rates for a single lump sum
of $37,483 at closing; a creditline of $37,483 - assuming half of it is taken at closing, and none thereafter;
and a monthly advance for life of $536.

---

*For the lump sum and creditline, the table is based on an initial rate of
10.56%, which is 5% more than the U.S. Treasury 1-year rate for
9/1/94. It is unlikely, however, that this initial rate will turn out to be
the annual average rate charged on the loan balance. So the TLCs are
based on an expected annual average rate of 12.21%. The difference
between initial and expected rates (1.65%) is the difference between
the 1-year and the 10-year Treasury rates for 9/1/94. This is the same
estimation method as the one used in the HUD/HECM program.

144

*Table 19: TLC Rates on a HomeFirst Loan to a
75-Year-Old Borrower in a $150,000 Home**

	At End of Year	TLC when annual average home appreciation equals		
		0%	3%	6%
LUMP SUM	2	18.4%	18.4%	18.4%
	7	14.1	14.1	14.1
	12	11	13.3	13.3
	17	7.8	10.7	13
	22	6	9	11.9
CREDIT-LINE	2	23.8%	23.8%	23.8%
	7	15.5	15.5	15.5
	12	14.1	14.1	14.1
	17	11.9	13.6	13.6
	22	9.2	12.1	13.3
MONTHLY LIFETIME	2	88.2%	98.6%	107.8%
	7	19.6	23.6	27.4
	12	9	13.9	17.5
	17	2.7	7.9	12.4
	22	-0.1	5.3	9.8

*See note at bottom of page 144.

HomeFirst Leftovers

Table 20 shows how much cash would be left if a HomeFirst loan ended at various points in the future. It's based on the same basic assumptions used to make **Table 19.**

For a discussion of the basic patterns in **Table 20**, see pages 115-116. If you select monthly advances for life, however, the discussion on those pages does not tell the full story.

Plus the Annuity

The amounts of leftover cash in **Table 20** include only the cash left over after the home is sold and the loan is repaid. So they only show what would be left if the loan is repaid upon your death.

If you sell and move, by contrast, you would continue to receive $536 each month from the annuity. **Table 20** does not reflect this fact. But the annuity would pay you a total of $6,432 each year for as long as you live - wherever you live.

So you have to consider this important fact when you evaluate the leftover cash from this plan. In fact, the continuing monthly cash may be very important to you if you do sell and move. It might even make it possible for you to consider selling and moving.

In **Part THREE**, you will see how the *total* of leftover equity plus the value of the continuing annuity compares from one plan to another.

146

*Table 20: Leftover Equity on a HomeFirst Loan to a
75-Year-Old in a $150,000 Home*

		Leftover equity when annual average appreciation equals		
	At End of Year	0%	3%	6%
LUMP SUM	2	$85,475	$93,971	$102,717
	7	39,597	71,664	109,853
	12	0	14,774	96,581
	17	0	0	36,926
	22	0	0	0
CREDIT- LINE	2	$109,483	$117,979	$126,725
	7	84,399	116,466	154,655
	12	38,352	97,746	179,553
	17	18,742	44,897	189,967
	22	18,742	18,742	161,853
MONTHLY LIFETIME*	2	$104,362*	$108,107*	$111,963*
	7	42,649*	56,785*	73,621*
	12	0*	0*	18,888*
	17	0*	0*	0*
	22	0*	0*	0*

Leftover equity equals home value minus total amount owed minus cost
of selling home, assumed to be 7% of the home's value. Also *includes
remaining creditline assumed to be withdrawn just prior to maturity.*
*Does not include continuing monthly advance ($536) from annuity.

Other HomeFirst Features

This loan generally becomes due and payable when you die, sell your home, or permanently move.

You must get HomeFirst's consent to be absent from the home for more than 2 consecutive months, or for more than 6 months in any one-year period. If it is medically determined that you cannot return to your home, the loan must be repaid.

The HomeFirst loan also may become due and payable if you

- ✓ fail to pay your property taxes or any special assessments;

- ✓ fail to maintain your homeowner's insurance;

- ✓ fail to keep your home in reasonable condition;

- ✓ rent some of your home to more than a single person or family or on more than a month-to-month basis, or change the use of the premises.

Lender Default

Like other reverse mortgages, the HomeFirst plan is subject to state laws on breach of contract, including remedies for the borrower and penalties to the lender.

In addition to these laws, the HomeFirst contract provides a penalty if the lender fails to advance loan funds to you as promised within 15 days of being notified by you via certified mail that loan advances have not been received.

If this happens, the lender may not charge interest on the loan balance - but may charge "shared appreciation" (if included in the contract) - for the period during which loan advances were not made.

This contractual penalty may become ineffective, however, if the total amount you owe reaches your loan's nonrecourse limit. After that point, it may not be possible to charge additional interest if the interest exceeds the limit. So this penalty may effectively phase out at that time.

HomeFirst Summary

The Transamerica HomeFirst plan

✓ is available in California, New Jersey, New York, and Pennsylvania, and expected in other states during 1995;

✓ offers a simple creditline based on equity amounts up to $600,000; and

✓ also offers monthly advances for life with an optional creditline or lump sum.

Chapter 14

The Freedom Plan

In the summer of 1993, a unique program was introduced through the joint sponsorship of an old company and a new company.

The old company - Union Labor Life Insurance (ULLICO) - is a $2 billion, labor-owned financial institution that has been providing financial services to labor unions and their members for over 65 years. The new company - Freedom Home Equity Partners - was formed to develop new reverse mortgage products.

The Freedom plan can provide substantial cash benefits. But it also can be *extremely expensive - OR quite inexpensive - depending on how long you live.* So before signing up for this program, be sure you understand its unique features.

Where and Who

By late 1994, the Freedom plan was available in California only. But during 1995, the program is expected to expand into other states.

To qualify for the Freedom plan,

✓ you do *not* have to meet an age requirement (although lower ages will generate smaller benefits);

✓ at least one owner must live in your home as a principal residence;

✓ your home may be a single-family dwelling, duplex, triplex, 4-unit building, condominium, or part of planned unit development (PUD).

Freedom Benefits

The Freedom plan lets you take all the money available to you as

☐ a single lump sum of cash,

☐ a monthly cash advance for as long as you live - *no matter where you live;* or as

☐ a combination of a lump sum plus a monthly advance for life.

How It Works

At closing, you get a large lump sum of cash. You may use all or some of it to purchase an "immediate" annuity. The annuity provides a monthly cash advance beginning immediately at closing, and continuing for the rest of your life.

Annuity Choices

You may buy the annuity from Metropolitan Life (Met Life) or Union Labor Life (ULLICO). The monthly advances from ULLICO are a bit larger. But Met Life is ranked much higher by the agencies that rate the financial strength of such companies.

The annuities from both companies come in several varieties. All provide a partial cash refund to your estate if you die within four years of closing. Some also provide continuing monthly payments to your estate for a certain period of time. These are known as "period certain" payments.

In general, the greater the cash to be paid to your estate, the smaller the monthly advance paid to you will be during your lifetime. The greatest monthly advances are paid when there are no "period certain" payments.

Equity Conservation Choices

The Freedom plan lets you choose how much of your equity to put into the deal, and how much you want left when it's over. This "equity conservation" feature is unique to the Freedom plan.

Here's how it works in general. At closing, you select a "lending value" (LV) percentage that limits your debt. For example, if you choose 60%, then in most cases

✓ you will never owe more than 60% of your home's value at the time the loan is repaid; and

✓ you - or your estate - will retain at least 40% of your home's value.

The greater the LV percentage you choose, the more money you can get in a lump sum or monthly advance. The LV percentage must be at least 25%. But it may not be greater than 75%.

How Much You Get

The amount of your lump sum advance is based on your age, the value of your home, the LV percentage you select, whether you are a single or a joint borrower, and the total of all loan fees and third-party closing costs.

The amount of your monthly advance depends on how much of the lump sum you decide to spend on an annuity, the company you buy the annuity from, the type of annuity you buy, and when you buy it. For example, if your loan closes when interest rates in general are high, then your annuity will pay you more than when interest rates are low.

Tables 21 and **22** show how much you can get.

*Table 21: Freedom Benefits for **Single** Borrowers at
Various Home Values and Ages**

HOME VALUE	AGE	Lump Sum Advance at Closing	Monthly Advance for Life
$150,000	65	$48,334	$372
	70	56,280	487
	75	64,664	647
	80	72,947	873
	85	77,952	1,163
	90	83,067	1,517
$200,000	65	$64,639	$498
	70	75,234	651
	75	86,412	864
	80	97,457	1,167
	85	104,131	1,554
	90	110,950	2,026
$250,000	65	$80,945	$623
	70	94,188	815
	75	108,161	1,083
	80	121,967	1,461
	85	130,309	1,944
	90	138,833	2,536

* The amounts in this table were the amounts available in the Fall of 1994. The monthly amounts assume annuities with no "period certain" payments to your estate.

*Table 22: Freedom Benefits for **Joint** Borrowers at Various Home Values and Ages**

HOME VALUE	AGE	Lump Sum Advance at Closing	Monthly Advance for Life
$150,000	65	$38,128	$258*
	70	45,663	336*
	75	53,959	443*
	80	62,708	596*
	85	71,159	810
	90	78,578	1,099
$200,000	65	$51,031	$345*
	70	61,078	449*
	75	72,140	593*
	80	83,805	796*
	85	95,072	1,083
	90	104,965	1,469
$250,000	65	$63,934	$432*
	70	76,493	563*
	75	90,321	742*
	80	104,902	997*
	85	118,986	1,356
	90	131,352	1,837

* The amounts in this table were the amounts available in the Fall of 1994. The monthly amounts assume annuities with no "period certain" payments to your estate, except *for couples under the age of 85, the annuities include a 4-year period certain.

Freedom Costs

Traditional types of itemized costs are not used in determining the total amount owed on a Freedom loan. Instead, a "percent of value" formula is used. Simply put, you end up owing some percent of your home's value.

Percent of Value

In most cases, the total amount you owe when the Freedom loan becomes due and payable is

♦ the home's value at that time,

♦ minus 7% of any increase in the home's value since closing,

♦ times the lending value (LV) percentage you selected at closing.

For example, assume you select an LV percentage of 75%, and your home is worth $150,000 at closing. If you die ten years later and your home's value has grown to $200,000, there would be $50,000 in appreciated value. So you would owe

♦ $200,000 minus $3,500 (7% of $50,000), or $196,500

♦ times 75%, for a total of $147,375.

Two Exceptions

In some cases, however, the "percent of value" formula is *not* used. There are two exceptions:

- if your home's value decreases, you could owe *more* than the formula repayment;

- if the loan is repaid within four years after closing, you could owe *less* than the formula repayment.

A Minimum

A minimum repayment is due if your home's value decreases beyond a certain point.

The minimum is calculated in two steps. First, your home's value at closing is multiplied times the lending value (LV) percentage you select. Then this amount is reduced by a compounded annual rate of 3.75% for each year of your projected life expectancy.

For example, assume your age is 75, your home's value at closing is $150,000, you select an LV percentage of 75%, and the annuity tables say your life expectancy is about 12.6 years. Reduce $112,500 (75% of $150,000) by 3.75% annually for that period, and the result is your minimum payment: $69,456.

So if your home's value fell below about $92,600 (75% of which is $69,450), you would then owe the minimum payment of $69,456 rather than the amount generated by the "percent of value" formula.

A Maximum

The formula repayment is subject to a maximum during the first four years of the loan. This means you could end up paying less than the "percent of value" formula says if you repay your loan during that time.

The maximum repayment equals the minimum repayment plus 13% compounded annually. In the example on the last page, the minimum repayment on a $150,000 home (assuming a 75% lending value percentage) was $69,456.

Adding 13% to this amount each year generates the maximum repayments shown below. The table also shows the formula repayments assuming an annual appreciation rate of 3%.

At end of year	Formula Repayment	Maximum Repayment
1	$115,639	$78,485
2	118,872	88,688
3	122,202	100,218
4	125,631	113,246

During each of the first four years of the loan, the maximum repayment is less than the formula repayment. So you would pay the lesser amount if you were to repay the loan during this time. Technically, the lower repayment is made possible by a partial refund of the cost of the annuity.

Interesting TLC Rates

Considering the debt in the early years of the Freedom plan, you have probably already guessed that its monthly advances are *very expensive in the short run.*

What you may not have guessed is that they are *relatively inexpensive in the medium to long run.*

Table 23 projects Total Loan Cost (TLC) rates for Freedom lump sum and monthly advances. It is based on a 75-year-old borrower living in a $150,000 home. The monthly advances for life ($647) and the lump sum ($64,664) are taken from **Table 21**.

Very High - Then Much Lower

In the early years of monthly advances, Freedom's TLC rates are very high because the debt (including funds to purchase an immediate annuity) is very high relative to the cash you receive from the annuity.

But the TLCs come down over time at a fairly fast rate. They do so because the loan's non-recourse limit in this case is 75% of the home's value. In other words, the non-recourse limit is *less* than the net sale proceeds.

So the total amount you owe in the early years is much greater than in other plans. But the total amount you can ever owe is much less.

In short, the monthly advances are very expensive or relatively inexpensive - depending on how long you live in your home. The longer you do, relative to your life expectancy, the more quickly the TLC decreases.

160

Table 23: TLC Rates on a Freedom Loan to a 75-Year-Old Borrower Living in a $150,000 Home

	At End of Year	TLC when annual average home appreciation equals		
		0%	3%	6%
LUMP SUM	2	15.9%	15.9%	15.9%
	7	7.9	10.7	13.5
	12	4.6	7.4	10.2
	17	3.3	6.1	8.9
	22	2.5	5.3	8.1
MONTHLY LIFETIME	2	146.7%	146.7%	146.7%
	7	18.7	23.2	27.6
	12	3	8	12.6
	17	-1.9	3.5	8.3
	22	-4.1	1.8	6.6

Freedom Leftovers

Table 24 shows how much cash would be left if a Freedom loan ended at various points in the future. It's based on the same general assumptions used to make **Table 23.**

For a discussion of the basic patterns in **Table 24**, see pages 115-116. For an important discussion about why this table does not tell the full story, see page 146.

In short, the latter discussion reminds you that if you sell and move, you would continue to receive $647 from the Freedom annuity each month ($7,764 per year) for the rest of your life *in addition to* the amounts in **Table 24** - which only show what's left after paying off the loan and selling the home.

In **Part THREE**, you will see how the *total* of leftover equity plus the value of the continuing annuity compares from one plan to another.

Also, if you take out the Freedom loan as a couple under the age of 85 and select monthly advances, you get four-year "period certain" advances at no extra cost.

This means that if you die within the first four years of the loan, your estate would continue to get monthly advances until the four-year period is over. So this would increase the amount of leftover cash as well.

Equity Conservation

Table 24 assumes you select a 75% "lending value" (LV) to get the greatest possible benefits.

If you select a lower LV percentage, your lump sum or monthly advances would be smaller. But the amount of leftover equity would be greater.

*Table 24: Leftover Equity on a Freedom Loan to a
75-Year-Old in a $150,000 Home*

	At End of Year	Leftover equity when annual average appreciation equals		
		0%	3%	6%
LUMP SUM	2	$50,812	$59,308	$68,054
	7	27,000	35,016	44,564
	12	27,000	41,849	62,300
	17	27,000	49,768	86,036
	22	27,000	58,949	117,798
MONTHLY LIFETIME	2	$50,812*	$59,308*	$68,054*
	7	27,000*	35,016*	44,564*
	12	27,000*	41,849*	62,300*
	17	27,000*	49,768*	86,036*
	22	27,000*	58,949*	117,798*

Leftover equity equals home value minus total amount owed minus the
cost of selling the home, which is assumed to be 7% of the home's
value.
*Does not include the value of the continuing monthly advance ($647)
from the annuity.

The Freedom plan's unique "equity conservation"
feature lets you decide how much equity to convert
into cash, and how much to conserve for the future.

Other Freedom Features

This loan generally becomes due and payable when you die, sell your home, or permanently move.

You must get the lender's consent to be absent from your home for more than 90 consecutive days. If you are absent for 375 days in any 475-day period, the loan becomes due.

The Freedom loan also may become due and payable under other circumstances that are spelled out in the loan documents. These conditions and situations include the following:

- ✓ you fail to pay your property taxes or any special assessments;

- ✓ you fail to maintain your homeowner's insurance;

- ✓ you fail to keep your home in reasonable condition;

- ✓ you rent some of your home to a third party on more than a month-to-month basis;

- ✓ you declare bankruptcy or insolvency; or

- ✓ you live in your home for more than 38 years without extending the loan.

Lender Default

Like other reverse mortgages, the Freedom plan is subject to state laws on breach of contract, including remedies for the borrower and penalties to the lender.

But remember that you are not dependent on a lender for making monthly payments to you in this plan. In the Freedom plan, you get a large lump sum of cash at closing. So you get all the money you're going to get from the lender at that time.

If you want monthly advances, you use some or all of the lump sum to purchase an annuity. So your monthly payments are the responsibility of the company that sells you the annuity. And Met Life gets very high marks from annuity rating agencies.

Freedom Summary

The Freedom plan

✓ is available in California only, but is expected in other states during 1995;

✓ offers substantial lump sums or monthly advances for life;

✓ has TLC rates on monthly advances that are *extremely expensive* in the short run, but *relatively inexpensive* in the medium to long run.

165

Chapter 15

The Fannie Mae Plan

You might be surprised to see even a short chapter about a reverse mortgage that may not yet exist.

But that's what you're looking at.

The Federal National Mortgage Association - also known as "Fannie Mae" - is expecting to introduce a new reverse mortgage program during 1995.

Fannie Mae had not completed its plan by the time this book went to press. But it had made public the general features of the plan it expected to offer.

Who Is Fannie Mae?

The Federal National Mortgage Association is the nation's largest supplier of home loan funding. It buys home mortgages from originating lenders, and sells them to investors.

This "secondary" mortgage market makes it possible for local lenders to make as many mortgages as consumers in their areas need.

HECM Angel

Fannie Mae was an early proponent of the reverse mortgage concept. In 1982, it supported a proposal of the National Center for Home Equity Conversion to create a federal reverse mortgage insurance program.

Since that program started, Fannie Mae has been its most important backer. It has purchased almost all the reverse mortgages made by HUD/HECM lenders. Without Fannie's funding, the HECM program would not be so widely available today.

HECM Analyst

Through its close involvement with the HUD program, Fannie has been able to analyze the benefits and limitations of the federally-insured plan first-hand.

Fannie Mae's experience with that program is what led it to develop its own reverse mortgage - a plan it expects will complement the HECM program.

168

What Will Fannie Offer?

Soon after it is introduced, Fannie Mae's new reverse mortgage is likely to become available on a broad national basis.

Most other reverse mortgages have been initially introduced into only one or a few states. Other than the HUD-HECM program, none have become available nationwide.

Because it will be offered through existing HECM lenders, Fannie's new product will probably spread to more states more quickly than any other reverse mortgage. That means it's quite likely to become a real option for you during 1995.

HECM Plus

In general, Fannie Mae's new reverse mortgage is expected to resemble the HUD-HECM program. Fannie's goal is a plan that

◆ offers a variety of cash advance options,

◆ but accepts more equity than HUD's 203-b limits allow.

The cash options are likely to include a lump sum, a creditline, monthly advances, and combinations of these three types of advances. At present, Fannie Mae's single national equity limit is $203,150.

Advance Amounts

The exact amount of the cash advances will not be known until the final details of Fannie's new plan are complete. But in general they are likely to be

✓ smaller than the HECM advances if your home's value is less or somewhat greater than HUD's 203-b limit in your area;

✓ but greater than the HECM advances if your home's value is substantially greater than HUD's 203-b limit in your area.

In short, the Fannie Mae plan will have a crossover point at which its cash benefits become greater than the HECM plan's.

Other Factors

In most other respects, the Fannie plan and the HUD plan probably will be quite similar.

◆ Fannie's itemized costs and TLC rates are likely to be somewhat greater than HUD's.

◆ Fannie cannot offer a federal loan guaranty, but it's a federally-chartered corporation and the nation's largest mortgage funder.

◆ Fannie probably will require some type of consumer education or counseling.

170

Keeping Posted

The best way to keep tabs on Fannie's progress is to be in touch with HUD-HECM lenders in your area.

Fannie Mae will provide information and training on its new reverse mortgage to these lenders before it begins offering the plan to the public.

So the HUD-HECM lenders will know that the Fannie plan is coming some time before it actually arrives.

Anticipating

Any smart shopper keeps alert to promising new products. The final details of Fannie's plan aren't yet available. But enough is known in general to keep it in mind as a possibility. Especially

✓ if you live in an area where only the HECM plan is currently available, and

✓ if your home is worth substantially more than HUD's 203-limit in your area.

Soon after the Fannie Mae program is unveiled, the National Center for Home Equity Conversion (see page 334) will publish a detailed analysis of the new plan.

Chapter 16

The Republic Plan

Here is another short "preview" chapter. (Nothing like knowing what's on the way.)

A new reverse mortgage plan is expected to be offered in 1995 by Republic Financial Corporation. Established in 1971, Republic is a Denver-based, private financial services organization. It provides financing for equipment leasing and real estate transactions.

By Fall of 1994, the Republic plan had been in development for nearly two years, and was expected to become available soon.

173

What's interesting about this new plan is that it is expected

✓ to be offered through an existing network of experienced reverse mortgage originators; and

✓ to include a new combination of reverse mortgage features.

An Old Network

Republic intends to offer its plan through the HUD/HECM lenders whose reverse mortgages are serviced by Wendover Funding (Greensboro, North Carolina).

As the largest reverse mortgage servicer in the nation, Wendover has developed a broad national network of reverse mortgage originators.

This means that the Republic plan may become more widely available more quickly than other plans have. If it does, it is more likely to become a real option for you in 1995.

A New Combination

Republic intends to combine a new mix of features in its forthcoming plan.

For example, it is likely to include

☐ monthly advances for life through a
deferred annuity (like the HomeFirst
plan), and

☐ an equity conservation feature (like
the Freedom plan).

The Republic plan may require that you take a
monthly advance. But it will permit you to take an
optional lump sum at closing in addition to the
monthly advance.

The dollar amount of the monthly advances is
expected to be roughly competitive with other plans.
The less equity you choose to conserve, the greater the
advances will be.

Because of the annuity and conservation features,
TLC patterns are likely to fall somewhere between the
cost patterns of the HomeFirst and Freedom plans.

In short, Republic expects its plan to be attractive
to persons

◆ who own homes worth more than HUD's
203-b limits;

◆ who are looking for monthly advances for life;
and

◆ who want to conserve some of their equity.

Keeping Posted

The HUD-HECM lenders in your area with servicing by Wendover should be the first to know when the Republic plan will become available.

Soon after the Republic program is launched, the National Center for Home Equity Conversion (see page 334) will publish a detailed analysis of the new plan.

Chapter 17

Fixed-Term Plans

The very first reverse mortgages made in the United States were simple "fixed-term" plans. Today, they are available in only a handful of places.

They are called "fixed-term" reverse mortgages because they must be repaid in full after a fixed term of years. In other words, they become due and payable on a specific date - or, if it is sooner, when you die, sell your home, or permanently move away.

These are the only reverse mortgages that do not safeguard your right to remain in your home for as long as you choose. But they can be a good choice in the right circumstances.

Where and Who

Most of the fixed-term programs began in the early to middle 1980s. Since then, only a few new ones have been developed. And many of the first plans no longer exist.

Fixed-term plans are available in Arizona, California, Maine, Massachusetts, Minnesota, New Jersey, New York, and Pennsylvania. See **Appendix B** and below for details.

Age Limits Vary

Eligibility criteria vary by program. In most plans there is a minimum age of 62 or 65. But a program in Southern California is limited to persons aged 72 and over. The only fixed-term plan in New Jersey, Pennsylvania, and most of New York (offered by Home-First) is limited to persons aged 90 and over.

For current details on qualifying for these loans, contact the specific programs listed in **Appendix B**.

Fixed-Term Benefits

Fixed-term reverse mortgages provide monthly loan advances for a fixed number of years - and then they must be repaid. In most plans, you select the length of the loan term. But there are usually limits on how long the term can be.

178

For example, some plans permit any length up to five years. Others limit the term to seven years, or to ten years. One plan permits any length *between* five and 12 years. Another offers only a 10-year term.

The length of the loan term is a key factor in determining the amount of your monthly loan advance. The shorter the term, the greater the monthly advances will be. Other factors are your home's value, the plan's "loan-to-value" limit, start-up costs, and interest rate.

Calculating the Advances

Here's how it works. The loan-to-value (LTV) limit is the largest balance the lender will permit at the end of the loan - expressed as a percentage of your home's value at closing.

If your home is worth $100,000 and the LTV limit is 70%, for example, then the monthly loan advance is the amount that would grow to reach $70,000 at the loan's repayment date.

If you select a 5-year term and the interest rate is 10%, the monthly advance is the amount that would reach $70,000 if it grew at 10% for five years.

Assuming that you pay your start-up costs out of pocket, that would be $896.49 per month.

In other words, if you charge 10% interest on a monthly loan advance of $896.49 for five years, the rising loan balance would reach $70,000 at the scheduled repayment date.

Financing Start-Up

If you finance your start-up costs, then you also must calculate what you would owe on that amount at the end of the term - and subtract it from the LTV limit. The result would be the amount you would use to calculate your loan advance.

For example, 10% interest charged on $3,500 in start-up costs would reach $5,758.58 in five years. So your loan advance would be the amount that would grow to $64,241.42 in five years: $822.74.

Adding a Lump Sum

If you want a lump sum at closing in addition to the monthly advance, you also must subtract its future value from the LTV. The method is identical to the one used above for financing start-up costs.

Advance Examples

Table 25 shows how much money you could get on a fixed-term reverse mortgage at 10% interest assuming various home values, LTV limits, and loan terms. The table also assumes that you finance all loan costs.

As you can see, greater home values generate greater monthly advances. Note also how much difference the LTV limit can make.

The key pattern in this table, however, is that the monthly advance is greater when the loan term is shorter. The monthly advance on a five-year term is substantially more than the advance on a 10-year term.

Table 25: Monthly Advances on a Fixed-Term Reverse Mortgage at 10% Interest*

Home Value	Loan-to-Value (LTV) Limit	Term (years)	Monthly Advance
$100,000	50%	5	$569
		10	198
	70%	5	825
		10	294
$150,000	50%	5	$859
		10	300
	70%	5	1,244
		10	445
$200,000	50%	5	$1,150
		10	403
	70%	5	1,662
		10	597
$250,000	50%	5	$1,441
		10	506
	70%	5	2,081
		10	748
$300,000	50%	5	$1,731
		10	608
	70%	5	2,500
		10	899

*Assumes financing of a 2% origination fee and closing costs totaling $1,400 on a $100,000 home, $1,800 on a $150,000 home, $2,200 on a $200,00 home, $2,600 on a $250,000 home, and $3,000 on a $300,000 home.

The main *benefit* advantage of a fixed-term reverse mortgage is that you can get a larger monthly advance by shortening the loan term.

At younger ages and shorter terms, this may lead to a greater advance than you could get from other programs. For example, you could get over $3,700 per month for two years if the LTV limit is 70% and your home is worth $150,000.

At older ages or longer terms, however, you might still get a greater advance from other programs. And remember, other plans do not require repayment when the monthly advances stop.

Fixed-Term Costs

Fixed-term loans generally have the same closing costs as other reverse mortgages. Most origination fees are 1% or 2% of home value, although one program charges a whopping 3.5%.

Interest rates are fixed for the life of the loan. At a time when the expected rate on the HUD/HECM loan was nearly 9%, the rate on fixed-term loans ranged from 8.5% to 11%.

The main *cost* advantage of these loans is that you don't have to pay an insurance premium or other risk-pooling charge. This lowers the overall start-up cost of the loan and, in most cases, the TLC rates as well. **Table 26** gives you the details. It assumes a 2% origination fee and $1,800 in closing costs.

Table 26: TLC Rates on Fixed-Term Reverse Mortgages Made on a $150,000 Home at 10% Interest at Different Loan-to-Value Limits and Loan Terms

	TLC when LTV Limit Is	
	50%	**70%**
At the end of a		
2-year term	17.6%	15.4%
7-year term	13.5%	12.4%
12-year term	13.3%	12.2%

TLC rates after two years are dramatically lower than those on other reverse mortgages providing monthly advances. With a 7-year term, the TLC is still lower. But if the loan term is 12 years, TLC rates are actually somewhat greater than on a comparable HECM loan, for example.

There are two reasons for this. First, the LTV limit on a fixed-term loan does not permit the loan balance ever to reach - and then be limited by - a non-recourse limit. (That's also why TLCs on a fixed-term loan do not vary by home appreciation rates.) Second, the monthly advances on a 12-year fixed-term loan are much smaller than similar advances on other loans.

TLCs are greater when the LTV is lower because a lower LTV generates smaller loan advances. And this increases the relative impact of the start-up costs.

Fixed-Term Leftovers

At the end of a fixed-term loan, your debt equals the loan-to-value (LTV) limit established at closing.

If the limit is 70%, for example, and your home was worth $100,000 at closing, then you would owe $70,000 when the loan becomes due and payable.

If your home's value does not increase during the loan term, and if the cost of selling your home is 7% of its value ($7,000), then you would have $23,000 in leftover equity at that time. In other words, even if your home does not appreciate, you would retain 23% of its value in remaining equity.

If your home does appreciate, your leftover equity would equal 93% of its value (assuming a 7% selling cost) minus $70,000.

Appreciation Matters

Table 27 shows the amount of remaining equity on various fixed-term loans with a 70% LTV limit. The home in each case is worth $150,000 at closing. The table shows leftover equity assuming three different appreciation rates.

As discussed above, if there is no appreciation, the amount of leftover equity is the same at the end of any term. The greater the appreciation rate, however, the more equity remains. And the longer the loan term, the greater difference the appreciation rate makes.

Table 27: Leftover Equity on Fixed-Term Reverse Mortgages Made on a $150,000 Home at 10% Interest with a 70% LTV Limit*

	Leftover equity when annual average home appreciation equals		
	0%	3%	6%
At the end of a			
2-year term	$34,500	$42,996	$51,742
7-year term	34,500	66,567	104,756
12-year term	34,500	93,894	175,701

* Assuming a 2% origination fee and $1,800 in closing costs.

Keep in mind that this table does not show leftover equity at various points on a single loan. Instead, it shows three different loans. The loan with a 2-year term, for example, provides much larger monthly advances ($3,718) than the loan with the 7-year term ($782) or the loan with the 12-year term ($321).

For Whom?

Now that you've seen the particulars, it should be clear that these loans have limited usefulness. Most people want the security of no repayment for as long as they live in their homes. And these loans do not provide that security.

185

But fixed-term reverse mortgages can be a reasonable choice *IF* you clearly intend or expect to sell your home or otherwise leave before the repayment date. *IF* you do, then you might conclude that the short-term cost savings are worth the added risk.

Assessing the Risk

The risk, of course, is that despite your present intentions or expectations, the future might unfold in some other way. You might end up wanting to remain in your home, but facing a repayment obligation that you can only meet by selling and moving.

If that happens, you might be able to pay off the fixed-term loan with another reverse mortgage. But whether you can do this will depend on how much your home has grown in value.

If you can refinance in this way, you may only be eligible for minimal monthly advances, or none at all. And you would have to pay the start-up costs all over again.

If you can only refinance with some other type of reverse mortgage, you also would end up paying an insurance premium or other risk-pooling fee after all.

Special Situations

Fixed-term reverse mortgages are most often used by very frail or sick persons who need expensive at-home help for the shortened life expectancies their doctors predict.

186

They have also been used by persons needing a short term income boost while planning to move. For example, persons

◆ on waiting lists for units in congregate housing facilities; or

◆ expecting to sell and trade down to lower-valued homes.

There may be other cases in which fixed-term loans are appropriate. In general, however, they have been used primarily in these types of situations.

Fixed-Term Summary

Fixed-term reverse mortgages

✓ must be repaid on a specific date;

✓ may offer larger monthly loan advances and lower costs when the fixed-term is short;

✓ may be appropriate for persons who intend to sell or leave their homes within a few years.

Chapter **18**

Public Sector Plans

If all you want is enough cash

✓ for home repairs or improvements, or

✓ to pay your property taxes,

then a public sector reverse mortgage may be your best choice.

Here are the three key features of these loans:

✓ They generally have lower costs than any other reverse mortgage.

✓ But the cash advance generally must be used for specific purposes.

✓ And you typically must have a low or moderate income to qualify for these loans.

Repairs and Improvements

Many local government agencies offer "deferred payment loans" (DPLs). This type of public sector reverse mortgage provides a one-time, lump sum advance that you must use to repair or improve your home. No repayment is required for as long as you live in your home.

Where and Who

DPLs aren't available everywhere, and they can be difficult to find. Your best bet is to contact your

✓ city or county housing department,

✓ area agency or county office on aging, or your

✓ community action or development agency.

Ask them about any home repair or improvement loans they offer. Tell them you're especially interested in any loans that don't have to be repaid until you die, sell, or move.

Eligibility criteria vary from program to program. Most are limited to homeowners with low or moderate incomes. Many place a limit on home value or location. Some have a minimum borrower age requirement.

DPL Benefits

DPLs can only be used for the specific types of repairs or improvements that each program allows. In many programs, this limits you to projects that replace or repair basic items such as your roof, wiring, heating, plumbing, floors, stairs, or porches.

Many programs also permit work that improves the accessibility or energy efficiency of your home. They may permit the installation of ramps, rails, grab bars, storm windows, insulation, or weatherstripping.

Less Cash

Generally, DPLs provide smaller lump sums than you could get from private reverse mortgages. How much smaller depends on the particular DPL program. It could well be a significantly smaller amount.

But you may be able to *combine* a DPL with a private plan - *if* the DPL lender agrees to be repaid *after* the private lender is repaid. This would give you a lower overall cost than a private loan alone.

191

DPL Costs

The best thing about DPLs is their very low cost. Generally they have no origination fee, no insurance premium, minimal - if any - closing costs, and very low - or no - interest.

If there is interest, it is most often charged on a fixed basis, that is, the rate never changes. The virtual absence of start-up costs means that the TLC rate on a DPL is basically the same as the loan's fixed rate.

Some DPL programs charge *simple* fixed interest. This means that interest is not charged on any of the interest that has been previously added to the loan balance. Simple interest also means that the TLC is *less* than the stated rate.

Some DPL programs even *forgive* part or all of the loan if you live in your home for a certain period of time after closing. In other words, you may end up paying nothing back - ever.

DPL Leftovers

If you are lucky enough to find and qualify for a "forgivable" DPL, you would most likely have more equity left at the end of the loan than you had at the beginning.

This could happen even if your loan isn't forgiven. For example, if you make an improvement that increases your home's value, that increased value could appreciate enough to pay back a 0% interest DPL.

Or enough to pay back part of an interest-bearing DPL. And that's like getting a discount on the improvement. If the increased value pays back half the loan, for example, that's like paying half-price for the improvement.

In any case, DPLs generally involve smaller lump sums and have very low costs. So they don't use up much equity. You get the benefit of a repaired or improved home, and may wind up with nearly the same equity as if you hadn't taken out a DPL.

No matter how you slice it, a DPL is one of the best bargains you will find.

Property Tax Deferral

Some state and local government agencies offer "property tax deferral" (PTD) loans. This type of public sector reverse mortgage provides annual advances that can only be used to pay your property taxes. No repayment is required for as long as you live in your home.

Where and Who

PTD programs are available in all or parts of 15 states. If you live in one of the states listed on the next page, contact the local government agency to whom you pay your property taxes. They can tell you if the program is available in your area, and what you must do to qualify.

California*	Illinois*	Texas
Colorado	Maine*	Utah
Connecticut	Massachusetts	Virginia
Florida	New Hampshire	Washington*
Georgia	Oregon*	Wisconsin*

In states marked with an asterisk (*), PTD is available on a uniform, statewide basis. In the other states, the program may not be available in all areas, and it may not be the same in all the areas in which it is available.

Eligibility criteria vary considerably. Most PTD programs

☐ have a minimum age of 65, and

☐ are limited to persons with low or moderate incomes.

PTD Benefits

The amount of the annual advance is generally limited by the amount of your property tax bill for that year. Some programs limit the annual advance to some part of the tax bill or to a specific amount.

The total amount you can borrow over the life of a PTD loan is limited in most programs. In other words, you may become ineligible for additional annual advances at some point in the future.

Property taxes typically equal anywhere from about 1% to 3% of a home's value. This means that the annual advance on a $150,000 home, for example, might be as little as $1,500 or as much as $4,500.

PTD Costs

Like deferred payment loans, PTD loans generally charge no origination fee, no insurance premium, and minimal - if any - closing costs.

The interest rate is usually fixed, but it varies from program to program. It has ranged from about 6% to 8% in state-administered plans. In some cases, interest is charged on a simple basis, that is, no "interest on interest."

In most cases the TLC rate on PTD loans is the same as the stated rate because

◆ start-up costs are minimal or non-existent, and

◆ the rising loan balance is unlikely to reach the home's value because

  • the annual advance is a small percent of the home's value, and

  • PTD programs usually cut off eligibility for additional advances when the loan balance reaches a given per cent of your home's value.

If simple interest is charged, then the TLC rate is *less* than the stated rate.

PTD Leftovers

The amount of leftover equity on a PTD loan depends on a combination of factors: the current tax rate, future changes in the tax rate, the appreciation rate, the interest rate, and whether interest is charged on a simple or compound basis.

Table 28 shows the amount of remaining equity at 0%, 3% and 6% appreciation - assuming a fixed 2% tax rate on a $100,000 home and 7% compound interest on the loan balance.

Appreciation = Equity

You can see that the amount of leftover equity is greatest when home values grow the most.

At 6% appreciation, this PTD plan is actually a *rising* equity loan for the first 22 years. If there is no appreciation, on the other hand, you run out of left-over equity by the end of 22 years.

Advances May Cease

Table 28 assumes that eligibility for additional advances stops when the next advance would push the debt over 80% of the home's current value. This occurs at the end of 24 years when annual appreciation averages 3%, and at the end of 18 years when there is no appreciation.

If the eligibility cut-off point is less than 80% of current value, then you would become ineligible for additional advances at an earlier point. So check this feature closely.

Table 28: Leftover Equity on a Property Tax Deferral Loan at 7% Interest on a $100,000 Home with a Tax Rate of 2% at Various Appreciation Rates*

	When annual average appreciation is		
	0%	3%	6%
Leftover Equity at End of Year 2	$86,570	$92,048	$97,689
7	72,480	91,807	114,970
12	52,719	85,530	131,751
17	25,002	69,840	145,309
22	0**	39,850	150,973
27	0**	0**	141,048

* Leftover equity equals home value minus loan balance and the cost of selling the home, which is assumed to be 7% of the home's value.

** Assuming annual advances cease when loan balance reaches 80% of current value.

Other Public Loans

A handful of state housing finance agencies (HFAs) have offered a variety of reverse mortgage programs over the past decade.

In general, these plans have been short-lived. When the money set aside to fund them has run out, they have closed their doors to new borrowers.

At present, HFAs in Connecticut, Montana and New Hampshire are offering a kind of "split-term" reverse mortgage (see **Appendix B**). (The Connecticut plan is limited to persons who are no longer able to function on their own.)

A "Split-Term" Loan

These plans provide monthly advances that stop after a fixed period of time. But the loan does not have to be repaid for as long as you live in your home.

So there are two separate or "split" terms: a term of loan advances, and a term to maturity (that is, when the loan becomes due and payable). That's different from the "fixed-term" loans discussed in **Chapter 17**. In those plans, the term of advances and the term to maturity are the same, fixed period of time.

The cost of HFA split-term loans is generally very low. But the benefits may be very limited as well. Before signing up for one of these deals, ask a HUD counselor to show you what you could get from a comparable HECM loan.

You'll probably end up choosing between

☐ a lower cost HFA loan that provides limited benefits, and

☐ a higher cost HUD/HECM loan that provides a greater range of benefit choices and, perhaps, greater loan advances as well.

Public Sector Summary

In general, public sector reverse mortgages

✓ have lower costs than any other reverse mortgages;

✓ must be used for specific purposes such as repairing or improving homes or paying property taxes; and

✓ are only available to persons with low or moderate incomes.

Part
THREE

Nest Egg
Comparisons

Chapter 19

Homing In

In **Part ONE** you learned about reverse mortgages in general. In **Part TWO** you learned about the details of specific reverse mortgage plans. Now it's time to put what you've learned to work.

Do any of these plans make sense for you?

Part THREE helps you answer this question by discussing other options, posing some basic questions, and comparing how the different plans meet a variety of cash needs.

✓ **Chapter 20** takes you briefly through the options other than reverse mortgages that you should be considering.

✓ **Chapter 21** reviews basic issues that will help you figure out if reverse mortgage borrowing is right for you in general.

✓ **Chapter 22** prepares you for the detailed comparisons that make up most of **Part THREE**.

✓ **Chapters 23-26** compare how the plans meet the different types of cash needs:

- lump sums **(Chapter 23)**

- creditlines **(Chapter 24)**

- monthly advances **(Chapter 25)**

- combinations **(Chapter 26)**.

✓ **Chapter 27** gives you a final checklist of things to look out for.

By the time you finish **Part THREE,** you will be well-equipped to make important decisions about your new retirement nest egg.

So let's get on with it. We'll start by looking at the other choices you may have.

Chapter **20**

Other Choices

When facing a big decision, you need to identify and carefully weigh all the choices available to you.

This is especially important when considering a major housing or financial decision beyond middle age, when you may have less ability to recover from a decision that turns out poorly for you.

So it's important to identify all your options, and to consider even the ones you're pretty sure you'll never choose. Who knows?

✓ The choice that doesn't look so good at first just might - upon closer inspection - turn out to be the best one of all.

✓ You might discover choices you never knew existed.

✓ You may discover a *combination* of choices that works better than any single one.

✓ The choice you discover today that makes little sense today might be perfect at some time in the future.

But even if none of these things happen, it's still important to consider all your options seriously. Why? Because *the best way to understand and evaluate any single choice is in relation to its alternatives.*

Seriously considering all your options will help you see more clearly why it is that you prefer some to others. Only by looking each choice squarely in the face will you be able to see it - and all the others.

For example, you may have read this far primarily because you want to stay in your own home, and need more money to do so. But if you haven't already done it, you should still look into selling and moving. It will help you put your other options into perspective.

Selling and Moving

Do you have any idea

✓ how much money you could get by selling your home?

✓ what it would cost to buy and maintain or rent a new home?

✓ how much you could safely earn on sale proceeds not used for a new home?

Most importantly, have you looked into the other homes that might be available for you to buy or rent? Take a look. It's always helpful to know by seeing first-hand and in-person what you might be missing.

☐ You may find a community or an array of services that is much more attractive than you thought it could be.

☐ Or, you may only confirm what you were pretty sure of all along: that where you live now is easily the best place for you to be.

But no matter what you find, you'll have a much better idea of the overall costs and benefits of staying versus moving. That will give you a better sense of what's valuable to you. And that will make it easier for you to evaluate the cost of other options.

Selling and Staying

It is possible - but not easy - to sell your home and continue living in it. The two ways of doing this are with a *sale leaseback* or a *remainder interest sale*.

Sale Leaseback

Sale leasebacks involve the sale of your home to an investor who agrees to rent it back to you for the rest of your life. It's been especially hard to find this type of investor since 1986, when federal tax law changes made these deals much less attractive.

Remainder Interest

Selling a remainder interest means that the buyer becomes the owner upon your death. Until that time you retain ownership in the form of a "life estate."

Federal tax law treats this type of deal even less favorably than sale leasebacks or outright sales. Some nonprofit organizations solicit *donations* of remainder interests in exchange for current tax deductions. So it only makes sense if you are in an upper tax bracket *and* you want to give away some of your equity.

Staying and Not Selling

If you stay in your home and do not sell, you still have options other than reverse mortgages. Some provide cash, some provide services, and some provide both.

Area Agencies on Aging

You can learn about these programs through your **Area Agency on Aging (AAA)**.

Call **1-800-677-1116** between 9 AM and 8 PM Eastern time Monday through Friday. Tell them your postal ZIP code, and they'll give you the telephone number for your local AAA.

Your AAA can help you learn about programs such as Supplemental Security Income (SSI), Medicaid, property tax relief, and energy assistance. It also can tell you about a wide variety of services programs that are designed to help you stay in your home.

Other Sources

Here are three other important sources of information that may be helpful to you:

◆ The **National Association of Professional Geriatric Care Managers** provides referrals to private care managers who coordinate local services; **602-881-8008**.

◆ The **National Academy of Elder Law Attorneys** provides referrals for assistance on a variety of legal issues; **602-881-4005**.

◆ **Children of Aging Parents** provides information and support groups for adult children; **215-345-5104**.

Other Loans

You should consider a home equity loan

◆ *if* you have enough income to qualify,

◆ *if* you can easily afford the monthly payments it requires, and especially

◆ *if* you intend to sell and move within a few years.

If you can get low start-up costs, so much the better. But be sure to read the fine print.

✓ Is an annual "requalification" required? If it is, your loan could become due and payable if your income goes down (for example, upon the death of a spouse).

✓ What are your rights if you miss a monthly payment? Be sure you understand what would make your loan "delinquent" and what you would have to do to avoid foreclosure and the loss of your home.

An excellent consumer guide to home equity loans is available free from AARP Fulfillment, Box 3401, Lakewood CA 90801.

Ask for "Borrowing Against Your Home: The Risks, Pitfalls and Advantages of Home Equity Loans" (D12987).

Getting Serious?

As you consider all your options and learn about reverse mortgages, you may find yourself

☐ more seriously considering a reverse mortgage, or even

☐ leaning toward a reverse mortgage.

If that's the case, you need to take two major steps before arriving at a final decision.

Most of **Part THREE (Chapters 23-26)** compares how the different reverse mortgages meet a variety of income needs. That's important because you need to figure out which plan does the best job of meeting your specific needs.

Getting Serious

But first you should step back and take another look at the general concept of reverse mortgages. A specific plan might meet your financial needs just fine. But how do you *feel* about reverse mortgages in general?

Are you comfortable with the idea? Do you have any nagging doubts? Does it go against any of your values? Or any of your attitudes about debt, saving, or risk?

The next chapter explores these issues.

Chapter 21

Back to Basics

We all have our own values, attitudes, and beliefs. They got us where we are in life. And generally we're not about to change them.

But the world around us changes. New products come along. We learn how to use them, and they improve our lives.

Sometimes, the improvements lead us to rethink things. We find that rules we've lived by may not apply to all new situations. Or that they may apply in different ways.

Examining the Rules

How do you really feel about debt and saving?

Most of us are reluctant to go into debt or spend our savings. We have grown up with these attitudes, and they have served us well.

So we are naturally cautious about any proposal to take on new debt or use our savings. And a reverse mortgage involves both.

Do reverse mortgages violate the financial attitudes or cautionary "rules" we've lived by? Let's take a closer look at three basic attitudes:

- ◆ "don't borrow in general"

- ◆ "don't borrow against your home in particular"

- ◆ "don't spend your savings."

We all violate these "rules" at some time. But we generally do so only for good reasons. The "rules" are really cautions. They make us think hard and carefully about what we're doing. And that can keep us from making major financial decisions we may later regret.

So let's look at the reasoning behind these rules. Does the logic apply to reverse mortgages? Does it apply in the same way as it does to other kinds of debt? In other words, can you take out a reverse mortgage without violating the spirit of these rules?

214

"Don't Borrow"

Borrowing usually means using money you haven't *earned* yet. You borrow today in the hope that you will be able to *earn* enough in the future to repay it.

So you are borrowing against your uncertain future earnings - which sounds like "counting your chickens before they hatch." And that's generally not a good idea unless you have a steady job and good prospects.

In Reverse?

But the basic logic of this rule doesn't apply to reverse mortgages because you are *not* borrowing against future income. In fact, you are borrowing against home equity that you have *already earned*.

So you aren't counting your chickens before they hatch. You are hatching the nest egg you've already earned.

"Not Against Your Home"

Borrowing against your home usually means paying back a loan every month. But if you lose your job or your income drops, you could miss some payments and lose your home to foreclosure.

That's why it's generally not a good idea to borrow against your home unless it's for a very basic purpose - such as buying, repairing, or improving it. Some people also borrow to finance a child's education, start a business, or refinance other debt. But the general rule is to avoid jeopardizing your home ownership.

In Reverse?

The logic of this rule doesn't apply to reverse mortgages either, because no monthly repayment is required.

You can't lose your home by missing a payment because there are none to make. Repayment comes when you die, sell your home, or permanently move away. And at that time the debt is limited to the net proceeds from the sale of your home.

"Don't Spend Your Savings"

"You don't know how much you will need and how long you will live. So don't spend your savings. Keep your powder dry. Keep saving for the future."

This rule has a lot of appeal. It urges you to be careful and cautious with your hard-earned savings. And that's proper.

After all, the only way you build up any savings is by keeping at it and resisting the urge to use the money too soon. So the rule is a helpful one for building up savings in the first place.

Never Ever?

But if you literally follow this rule forever, you would never use any of the money you've spent a lifetime building up.

That doesn't make much sense, does it? Why go to the trouble of earning it and saving it if you're never going to use any of it?

216

The Retirement Version

Once you've reached retirement, therefore, the rule changes. The caution is still there. But now the issues are different:

✓ when should I use savings?

✓ how much should I use?

✓ what should I use it for?

You still have to be cautious, however. Because the more you use now, the less you'll have later. So you still have to be concerned about

☐ how much you will need,

☐ when you will need it, and

☐ how long you will need it.

In Reverse

In this revised sense, the rule clearly does apply to reverse mortgages. Remember, it's these new loans that make your home equity "savings" usable.

Before reverse mortgages, most people never had to think about using their home equity savings. They didn't want to move and they didn't want the burden of monthly loan payments. So they just kept on saving their home equity until death.

Now that has changed. Now you can decide to use your home equity. So you aren't forced to keep on saving for lack of an alternative.

The revised, retirement version of the rule leads to questions such as

- ◆ Should you take out a reverse mortgage now?

- ◆ Or wait until later to decide?

- ◆ If you take one out now, how much of your equity should you take as

  - • a lump sum at closing,

  - • a monthly advance, or

  - • a creditline?

Aid to Planning

Remember, taking out a reverse mortgage does not require that you use all of your home equity now.

If you choose a monthly advance, you continue getting cash on a regular basis for as long as your plan provides. So you would be converting your equity into a new source of *continuing* income.

And if you choose a creditline, *you retain control over when and how much of your equity you use.* So you would still be able to "keep your powder dry" until you decide to use it. Creditlines *reposition* your equity so it's there when you need it.

218

Reviewing the Exam

Reverse mortgages do not violate the cautionary spirit of the three rules we have just examined.

The logic of the first two does not even apply to reverse mortgages. And the sense of the third reminds us to be prudent when using our home equity savings.

Yes, you could use a reverse mortgage unwisely. At age 62 with low income and few other assets, you could spend a lot of money foolishly or wastefully in the very first year - and then have much less to fall back on when you really need it.

But you also can be very careful and deliberative in making decisions about using reverse mortgages. It's up to you. Anyone who has read this far undoubtedly qualifies as a careful planner. And that's what the third "rule" on savings is all about.

So let's move on to the basic questions that will help you decide if a reverse mortgage makes sense for you.

Analyzing the Questions

The two main questions that any potential reverse mortgage borrower should consider are these:

✓ Can I get what I need?

✓ Am I willing to pay for it?

Meeting Your Need

Why are you looking into reverse mortgages? What need do you hope a reverse mortgage can fill?

- ◆ Do you want to replace high-interest "forward" debt that you must repay every month with "reverse" debt that requires no monthly repayment?

- ◆ Are you having trouble making ends meet every month?

- ◆ Are you doing OK most months, but having trouble with irregular expenses?

- ◆ Do you have a specific major need such as a home repair or improvement?

- ◆ Are you trying to pay for in-home care or other services to help you remain independent?

- ◆ Are you doing fine now, but concerned about your ability to meet changing financial needs in the future?

- ◆ Are you financially secure, and just want to use some of your equity to better your life?

No matter why you are interested in reverse mortgages, you should first figure out if any of them can meet your needs.

Chapters 23-26 compare how the different types of reverse mortgages meet a variety of income needs. This analysis will tell you if your specific cash needs can be met with a reverse mortgage.

It may be that your needs simply cannot be met with a reverse mortgage of any kind. If that's the case, go back to **Chapter 20**, and re-evaluate the other choices that may be available to you. On the other hand, your needs might be met if you wait a while (see "Now or Later?" on the next page).

Available to You?

You may find a specific reverse mortgage program that meets your needs but

☐ it may not yet be available in your area, or

☐ you may not qualify for it.

Reverse mortgages tend to become available first in the largest states with the highest concentrations of older homeowners. If you live in small or sparsely-populated state, your options may be limited now. The HECM plan may be the only one available at present.

When the Fannie Mae plan is unveiled, it should become available on a broad national basis rather quickly. The other plans probably will take longer to reach the less densely-populated states. One way to see if these plans are available in your area is to call their "800" numbers listed in **Appendix B**.

If your property does not qualify for one plan, it may for another. If you do not qualify by age, you may have to wait until you are older. But if you face a true emergency, you might consider a home equity loan now that can be refinanced with a reverse mortgage later.

This could be very costly, however, because you would end up paying all the start-up costs twice. In addition, much of the reverse mortgage would be used up in paying off the home equity loan balance.

Now or Later?

*A key question for anyone seriously considering a reverse mortgage is "when?". **If you are going to do it, should you do it now or later?***

In the future, you may well be eligible for much larger cash advances. At that time you will be older, and your home most likely will be worth more.

When you look at the various tables comparing cash advances in **Chapters 23-26**, be sure to check out *how much more* you could get if your age and home value were greater.

If interest rates or other costs are lower in the future, your cash advances would be greater still. On the other hand, if your home's value falls or interest rates or loan costs rise, your cash advances could end up lower despite your greater age.

The future is likely to bring you a wider array of reverse mortgage choices. So if your needs aren't met by today's plans, they may be met by tomorrow's.

222

If you are newly or not yet retired, you might start thinking about reverse mortgages as a kind of backstop to your future cash needs.

For example, you could plan your retirement budget without taking your home equity into account. Then, if you or your surviving spouse ends up living longer than expected, or if you otherwise encounter unexpected cash needs, you could consider a reverse mortgage at that time.

That's what having a nest egg is all about. You don't use it till you need it. But until that time, you know it's there.

Evaluating the Cost

If you are eligible for a reverse mortgage that meets your needs and is available in your area, the next question is: are you willing to pay for it?

Only you can answer this question. Because only you know what it is worth to you to meet your needs. Only you know how valuable it is to you

- ◆ to remain living in your own home,

- ◆ to pay off a debt that requires monthly repayments,

- ◆ to repair or improve your home,

- ◆ to increase your monthly income,

223

◆ to have a cash reserve (creditline) for
   irregular or unexpected expenses,

◆ to get the services you need to remain
   independent, or generally

◆ to improve the quality of your life.

All of these sound very good, of course. But how
much would you really be willing to pay to have any
of these needs met?

Answering this question is not as simply done as
making other cost decisions. As you have learned,
evaluating the cost of a reverse mortgage is much
different from most other cost assessments.

Little or No Cash

You don't have to reach very deep into your
pocket to pay for a reverse mortgage. Because you
can finance most of the start-up costs with the loan,
you don't have to use much current income or savings
to get it.

That makes it much easier to sign up for a reverse
mortgage. The current cash cost to you is very low.
But just because you are financing many of the costs
doesn't mean you aren't paying them.

On the other hand, if your rising loan balance
eventually reaches your loan's nonrecourse limit, you
will in effect end up paying much less - or in some
cases nothing - in start-up costs.

Total Cost Variations

Total Loan Cost (TLC) rates on a reverse mortgage can vary tremendously. Depending on how long the loan runs and how much your home's value changes, the real cost to you could be very high or very low.

So how can you figure out if you're willing to pay when you can't know for certain what it will cost? About all you can do is

☐ eyeball the loan's TLC table,

☐ get a sense of the *range* of potential costs, and

☐ ask yourself if you're willing to pay the TLC rates most likely to occur.

If you end up living in your home a long time, you could get a true bargain. But if you die, sell, or permanently move within just a few years, the true cost to you could be extremely high.

There's no way of avoiding this fundamental risk. You just have to understand it in general, assess the potential TLCs, and make your decision.

Start by assuming you will live in your home to about your life expectancy and your home will appreciate at a moderate rate (for example, 3%). Then ask yourself:

Is the cost of this "most likely" case acceptable considering how much I value what this deal will do for me compared to my alternatives?

Then look at the potential higher costs if you live for a longer time or your home appreciates more. Are you willing to take on the risk of higher cost?

Now consider the potential lower costs if you live less than average or your home appreciates at less than a moderate rate. Does that possibility seem likely to you? Does it offset the risk of higher costs?

Just remember, TLCs are not really comparable to the rates quoted on forward mortgages because

✓ TLC rates include *all* the costs;

✓ reverse mortgages require no monthly repayments;

✓ reverse mortgages can provide an open-ended monthly income guarantee, or a guaranteed creditline (which may grow larger); and

✓ you can never owe more than your home is worth, even if its net value is less than what your loan balance would otherwise have been.

Greater Cost = Less Equity

At this point you might be thinking, "Who cares what it costs?"

You might figure the odds are that the loan will be repaid after you're gone. So you might not care what it ends up costing so long as your needs are met during your lifetime.

226

There is some merit to that idea, especially if you have no heirs, or if your heirs are doing just fine. But keep in mind that the more equity that goes to the lender as costs, the less will be left for you if you do sell and move.

Remember also that plans with the highest cost in the early years of the loan may have the lowest cost in the later years. So you have to consider both the short-term and the long-term risks of high loan costs.

On to the Details

This chapter has considered some basic questions about reverse mortgages in general. Now you need to compare the specific details of individual reverse mortgage programs.

Chapters 23-26 provide these comparisons. But first, the next chapter shows you how the comparisons will be made.

Chapter 22

Making Comparisons

How do the reverse mortgages you learned about in **Part TWO** compare?

As you probably already suspect, a lot depends on how the comparisons are made. Unless you take care to compare "apples to apples" you will end up with misleading information.

That's why this chapter reviews the ground rules for comparing reverse mortgages. It starts off with a brief recap of the plans you have learned about.

Recapping the Plans

For a quick review of the reverse mortgages you met in **Part TWO**, turn back to pages 91 and 93. The tables on those pages summarize the basic benefit and cost features of these plans. Wander through the overview these tables provide.

Remember?

- ◆ Currently-available, multi-purpose plans offered by private sector lenders:

    - the HUD/HECM plan,

    - the Household plan,

    - the HomeFirst plan, and

    - the Freedom plan.

- ◆ Soon-to-be-available, multi-purpose plans offered by private sector lenders:

    - the Fannie Mae plan, and

    - the Republic plan.

- ◆ Plans with more limited cash benefits best suited for specialized needs and circumstances:

    - fixed-term plans, and

    - public sector plans.

Apples to Apples

Comparing a variety of plans requires careful attention to detail and a clear explanation of key assumptions. These involve closing costs, interest rates, non-recourse limits, creditline usage, and the types of cash advances a borrower selects.

Closing Costs

Third-party closing costs (not including origination fees) are typically the same for all reverse mortgages in a given area. They may differ a lot from one area to another. But all the loans made in the same area usually have roughly the same closing costs.

In calculating all the figures in **Chapters 23-26**, a uniform set of closing costs is used. These costs are based on approximate national averages determined by an informal survey of reverse mortgage lenders, as follows:

Home Value	Closing Cost Assumption
$50,000	$1,000
$100,000	$1,400
$150,000	$1,800
$200,000	$2,200
$250,000	$2,600

Interest Rates

As you learned in **Part TWO,** the interest rates charged on loan balances can differ from one plan to another. And many of the rates are tied to indexes that vary over time.

So the only way to get fairly comparable figures is to use the actual rates charged by each lender at the same point in time. Accordingly, all the figures in **Chapters 23-26** are based on the appropriate rates for September 1, 1994.

It is also necessary to adopt a consistent method for changing an adjustable initial rate to an expected rate. In **Chapters 23-26,** the difference between HUD's initial and expected rate for 9/1/94 (1.65%) is added to initial rates of other plans with adjustable rates. These assumptions produce the following rates:

REVERSE MORTGAGE	INITIAL RATE	EXPECTED RATE
HUD/HECM·	7.16%	8.81%
Household	10.75%	12.40%
HomeFirst		
Standalone Lump Sum or Creditline	10.56%	12.21%
Monthly Advances	9.75%	9.75%
Optional Creditline	12.50%	12.50%

Nonrecourse Limits

Most reverse mortgages specify that you can never owe more than the "net proceeds" from the sale of your home.

In **Chapters 23-26**, all TLC rate and leftover cash calculations are based on the assumption that the net proceeds equal 93% of the home's value. This leaves 7% of the home's value to pay for the costs of selling the home.

Advance Types

As you learned in **Chapter 6**, the pattern of Total Loan Cost (TLC) rates depends largely on the types of cash advances you choose.

TLCs on any reverse mortgage providing a single lump sum, for example, will be very different from those on any plan providing monthly advances.

Chapters 23-26 avoid this problem by consider one type of loan advance at a time.

Creditline Use

Chapter 6 also showed you that TLC rates on creditlines can vary tremendously, depending on

☐ how much money you take out, and

☐ when you take it.

So a fair comparison of two creditline products should assume the same usage pattern. Unless otherwise noted, in **Chapters 23-26** all TLCs are based on the assumption that you use one-half (50%) of an available creditline at closing, and none after that.

It's unlikely that you would use a creditline exactly in this way. But this analysis will show you how costs compare generally from one creditline plan to another.

Pre-Tax v. Post-Tax

Taxes are the one major factor that are *not* taken into account in the comparisons ahead.

The main reason is that this book does not provide legal or tax advice. Another reason is that current tax laws are subject to change. So your own legal advisor is your best source of information.

A third reason is that individual tax circumstances can vary so greatly from one consumer to another. This is especially the case when you use a very broad definition of taxes.

Broadly Defined

In the context of reverse mortgages, "taxes" may be broadly defined as *any government action that reduces the net benefits of a reverse mortgage.* In this sense, low-income borrowers are "taxed" if their receipt of cash advances leads to a loss of government benefits.

First, let's consider the "garden variety" taxes that are collected by the Internal Revenue Service (IRS). Then we'll look at potential benefit reductions and disqualifications involving government programs.

Federal Taxes

Three main areas of federal tax concerns are the taxability of cash advances paid to you, the deductibility of interest paid by you, and the potential for a net capital gains liability when the loan is repaid.

Taxability

The American Bar Association's 1992 edition of its **Attorney's Guide to Home Equity Conversion** (see **Resources,** page 328) states that generally "the IRS does not consider loan advances to be income."

But *annuity* advances are clearly another matter. Cash advances from an annuity *are* partially taxable. *So if you are considering a plan that includes annuity advances, you need to determine what your net cash advances would be after taxes.*

The figures in **Chapters 23-26** do not take the partial taxability of annuity advances into account. The amount of any tax will depend on your specific situation.

So remember that the annuity advances presented in these chapters are the *gross* annuities, that is, *before* taxes. This means that they may overstate the true benefit of these plans to you on an after-tax basis.

Deductibility

Interest is generally not deductible on your taxes until it is actually paid, according to the **Attorney's Guide to Home Equity Conversion**.

Reverse mortgage interest is added to your loan balance, but is not actually paid until the loan is over. At this time the accumulated interest is available as a deduction, subject to applicable IRS regulations.

The leftover cash figures in **Chapters 23-26** do not take interest deductibility into account. In fact, this interest is a kind of tax "asset" because it can be used to offset any taxes you owe.

Capital Gains

In theory, a "capital gains" tax may be due anytime a home is sold. The tax is based on increases in your home's value, minus certain adjustments like the cost of selling and home improvements. In practice, many of us never have to pay this tax.

- ◆ As long as you buy a new home of equal or greater value, you can postpone your gain.

- ◆ After age 55, you get a one-time "exclusion" that eliminates taxes on up to a $125,000 gain.

- ◆ If you remain in your home until death, your heirs get a "step-up in basis" that eliminates all prior gain (for spouses, the step-up may be total or partial depending on ownership status).

So if the last surviving reverse mortgage borrower dies before the home is sold, no capital gains tax is generally due. This is the most likely case.

But even if you do sell and move, you will still owe no tax if your gain is less than $125,000 and you have not already used the one-time exclusion.

If your gain is greater than $125,000 or if you have already used the exclusion, you can use your interest deductions to reduce or eliminate any tax owed. If you have used the loan to refinance or substantially improve your home, you may be eligible for greater interest deductions. (More on this in **Chapter 27.**)

The leftover cash figures in **Chapters 23-26** do not take potential capital gains (or alternative minimum) taxes into account. If you end up selling and moving before loan maturity, and if your interest deductions do not fully offset any tax due, then the leftover cash figures overstate your true net position at that time.

Government Benefits

Your Social Security and Medicare benefits are *not* affected by reverse mortgages. But some other government benefits might be. In general, they are the types of benefit programs in which eligibility is based on your financial situation.

If you get cash benefits from the Supplemental Security Income (SSI) program in particular, be sure to read this section carefully. Federal SSI rules are often used by other programs such as Medicaid.

In general, these types of programs count *loan* advances differently than *annuity* advances.

Loan Advances

In the federal SSI program, a *loan* advance cannot affect your SSI benefits if you spend the loan advance during the calendar month in which you get it.

On the other hand, if you keep the loan advance past the end of the calendar month (in a checking or savings account, for example), then it will count as a "liquid asset." If your total liquid assets at the end of any month are greater than $2,000 for a single person or $3,000 for a couple, you become ineligible for SSI.

So if you are an SSI recipient, be certain to get only as much in a reverse mortgage *loan* advance as you expect to spend within the month. Otherwise, you may lose your SSI benefits and any other benefits with similar eligibility rules. In most states, that includes the Medicaid program.

Annuity Advances

In the federal SSI program, an *annuity* advance directly affects your benefits.

In fact, ***the money you get from an annuity can reduce your SSI benefits dollar-for-dollar, or make you ineligible for Medicaid.***

So if you are considering an annuity-based plan, and if you are now receiving - or expect someday you may qualify for - SSI or Medicaid, be certain you fully understand the financial consequences in detail.

238

Check with the SSI, Medicaid, and other program offices in your community to find out how the receipt of *annuity* income would affect these benefits.

The figures in **Chapters 23-26** do not take the effect of such benefit reductions and eligibility disqualifications into account. In this sense, the figures may overstate the true impact of reverse mortgages that provide cash advances through annuities.

Comparisons On Tap

The next four chapters compare how the various plans meet four different types of income needs:

♦ lump sums **(Chapter 23)**;

♦ creditlines **(Chapter 24)**;

♦ monthly advances **(Chapter 25)**; and

♦ combinations **(Chapter 26)**.

Since all of these plans are subject to change, however, you should keep in mind that the precise details of the comparisons are tied to a specific date (9/1/94) and set of assumptions (discussed in this chapter).

Besides, your unique circumstances are bound to be different from the general assumptions used in the comparisons. For example, real closing costs will vary widely from the assumed costs.

Plans are subject to change, general assumptions vary over time, and your personal situation is not likely to be the norm.

But the basic methods of comparison demonstrated in these chapters will show you how to evaluate the competing claims of different programs

✓ at any time,

✓ under any set of assumptions, and

✓ as they apply to your situation.

Getting Started

So let's get into it. The next chapter considers the lump sums you could get from different plans.

You may not be interested in a single lump sum of cash. But take a look in any case. **Chapter 23** also provides a simple introduction to the comparison methods that will be used in the following chapters.

Chapter **23**

Comparing Lump Sums

Are you looking for a single lump sum of cash?

This chapter compares the largest possible lump sum advance that you could get from different reverse mortgage plans.

But first, we need to consider why you are looking for a single lump sum.

Why a Lump?

There are many reasons why you might be in the market for one large chunk of cash. Let's briefly look at a few of the more obvious ones.

Investing?

Maybe you are thinking about taking a large lump sum of cash and investing it.

If you are, forget it. Don't even think about it. You simply cannot safely earn a higher rate of return on your investment than you would pay in interest and other costs on your reverse mortgage. And you really can't afford to put your home equity at risk in the hope that you will get lucky.

Of course, *if* your home is just one of your many substantial assets and *if* you have way more net worth than you could ever possibly need and *if* you could easily afford to lose your lump sum investment and *if* you would be investing for purely recreational purposes, then you might consider it. But that's a lot of if's.

Depositing?

Maybe you are thinking about taking a large lump sum of cash and putting it in the bank. This would give you a nice reserve that you could use when you need it, you figure, and it would earn interest as well.

That might sound good. But if you think about it a bit, you'll see that it's generally not a very good idea.

Remember, you would be charged a higher rate of interest on the full amount of the lump sum loan than you would be earning on the bank account. So you would be losing money every month.

A creditline is generally a better alternative. You are *not* charged interest on the full amount of a creditline. Interest is charged only on each cash advance as and when you take it.

And some creditlines actually increase over time. So you get the same effect as "earning interest."

Paying Off?

Maybe you are thinking about using a large lump sum to pay off a large amount of debt. That would do away with your current monthly repayments on that debt, you figure, and leave you with more cash each month as a result.

This can be one of the very best uses of a lump sum. Especially if the debt is against your home, you have fallen behind on your payments, and are being threatened with foreclosure and the loss of your home.

But first you should consider all your options for getting out of the jam you are in. A *tremendously helpful* resource in this regard is an outstanding book published by the National Consumer Law Center called **Surviving Debt**. It's available for $15 postpaid from NCLC, 11 Beacon Street, Boston MA 02108.

In considering the best way of dealing with debt, keep in mind that a reverse mortgage does not require monthly repayments. So you wouldn't have to worry about falling behind again. And without monthly payments to make, you would have more cash left for other purposes each month.

Repairing or Improving?

Maybe you are thinking about using a large lump sum to make a major home repair or improvement.

If you are, you should first find out if any deferred payment loans (DPLs) are available in your area (see **Chapter 18**). If you qualify for one of these low-cost or no-cost loans, perhaps that is all you need.

If it isn't, you may still be able to get a private reverse mortgage in addition to the DPL. To do this, the DPL program must agree to let the private loan be repaid in full before the DPL is repaid. Many government agencies will agree to this "subordination" of their loan to a private reverse mortgage.

Lump Sum Benefits

So how much can you get from the reverse mortgages that let you take all your money as a single lump sum of cash?

Tables 29-30 compare the amounts you could get from four private sector programs in the Fall of 1994.

Table 29: Lump Sums for Single Borrowers from Four Reverse Mortgage Plans*

HOME VALUE	AGE	HUD/ HECM	HOUSE- HOLD	HOME- FIRST	FREE- DOM
$150,000	65	$43,079	$26,400	$19,583	$48,334
	70	52,604	33,100	27,788	56,280
	75	63,672	46,000	37,483	64,664
	80	75,711	57,000	48,155	72,947
	85	88,161	78,000	58,392	77,952
	90	100,487	92,300	68,562	83,067
$200,000	65	$43,864	$35,400	$26,579	$64,639
	70	53,537	44,300	37,499	75,234
	75	64,778	61,600	50,400	86,412
	80	77,003	76,200	64,598	97,457
	85	89,645	104,200	78,214	104,131
	90	102,158	123,200	91,738	110,950
$250,000	65	$43,864	$44,400	$33,576	$80,945
	70	53,537	55,600	47,210	94,188
	75	64,778	77,100	63,317	108,161
	80	77,003	95,400	81,040	121,967
	85	89,645	130,400	98,036	130,309
	90	102,158	154,200	114,915	138,833

*The lump sums in this table were available in the Fall of 1994. They assume financing of all loan costs, and are based on the interest rate assumptions discussed in **Chapter 22.**

*Table 30: Lump Sums for **Joint Borrowers** from Four
Reverse Mortgage Plans**

HOME VALUE	AGE	HUD/ HECM	HOUSE- HOLD	HOME- FIRST	FREE- DOM
$150,000	**65**	$43,079	$20,800	$19,583	$38,128
	70	52,604	26,400	27,788	45,663
	75	63,672	37,000	37,483	53,959
	80	75,711	46,000	48,155	62,708
	85	88,161	63,300	58,392	71,159
	90	100,487	78,000	68,562	78,578
$200,000	**65**	$43,864	$28,000	$26,579	$51,031
	70	53,537	35,400	37,499	61,078
	75	64,778	49,500	50,400	72,140
	80	77,003	61,600	64,598	83,805
	85	89,645	84,600	78,214	95,072
	90	102,158	104,200	91,738	104,965
$250,000	**65**	$43,864	$35,100	$33,576	$63,934
	70	53,537	44,400	47,210	76,493
	75	64,778	62,100	63,317	90,321
	80	77,003	77,000	81,040	104,902
	85	89,645	105,900	98,036	118,986
	90	102,158	130,400	114,915	131,352

*The lump sums in this table were available in the Fall of 1994. They assume financing of all loan costs, and are based on the interest rate assumptions discussed in **Chapter 22**.

Only the HUD plan is available in most states at present. In a few states you can choose between the HUD plan and one or (in California) two others. In no state can you currently choose from among all four plans. And, as the newer plans become available in more areas, the benefits they provide may change due to competition.

But the comparisons are interesting and instructive nonetheless. For example, they show you the importance of HUD's equity limits, the different ways in which joint borrowers are treated, and the variety in "tenure expectancy" assumptions.

HUD's Limits

You can see in **Tables 29-30** that the amounts available from the HECM program don't vary much with the value of your home.

The reason is that HUD's greatest 203-b limit is $152,363. So if your home is worth more, you can only get as much *as if* your home is worth $152,363.

The tables assume a limit of $152,363. But the limits are less than that in many areas. They can be as low as $77,197. *So the amount you can get from the HECM plan in your area could well be less than the amounts shown in Tables 29-30.*

Call a HUD lender in your area (see **Appendix B**) to find out how much you could get on your home in your area. It might make the amounts in the other plans look much better by comparison.

Joint Borrowers

A close reading of **Tables 29-30** also shows you that some plans have separate benefit schedules for single versus joint borrowers - and others don't.

In particular, the HECM and HomeFirst plans simply use the age of the youngest borrower when there is more than one. The Household and Freedom plans, by contrast, have a separate schedule for joint borrowers.

Tenure Expectancy

And did you notice that different plans apparently make much different assumptions about how long borrowers of various ages will live in their homes?

For example, the HUD and Household plans give smaller lump sums to singles aged 65 than the Freedom plan does. But they give greater lump sums to singles aged 90 than the Freedom plan does.

In other words, they are using different life expectancy tables or making different adjustments to the tables.

Lump Sum Costs

Table 31 compares TLC rates on lump sum loans to a 75-year-old borrower living in a $150,000 home. The figures come from the TLC tables on the various plans that you saw in **Part TWO**.

Table 31: TLC Rates on Lumps Sums from Four Reverse Mortgage Plans to a 75-Year-Old Living in a $150,000 Home*

	at end of year	Total Loan Cost Rate			
		HUD/ HECM	HOUSE HOLD	HOME- FIRST	FREE- DOM
Average	**2**	14.7%	17.4%	18.4%	15.9
Annual Home	**7**	11	13.8	14.1	7.9
Appreciation	**12**	6.6	9.3	11	4.6
= 0%	**17**	4.6	6.5	7.8	3.3
	22	3.6	5.1	6	2.5
Average	**2**	14.7%	17.4%	18.4%	15.9%
Annual Home	**7**	11	13.8	14.1	10.7
Appreciation	**12**	9.5	12.3	13.3	7.4
= 3%	**17**	7.6	9.5	10.7	6.1
	22	6.5	8	9	5.3
Average	**2**	14.7%	17.4%	18.4%	15.9
Annual Home	**7**	11	13.8	14.1	13.5
Appreciation	**12**	10.4	13.2	13.3	10.2
= 6%	**17**	10.1	12.4	13	8.9
	22	9.4	10.9	11.9	8.1

*The TLC rates in this table come from the TLC tables in **Part TWO**. They assume financing of all loan costs, and are based on the interest rate assumptions discussed in **Chapter 22**.

The range of projected TLC rates (from the highest to the lowest) is generally much smaller on lump sums than on other types of advances. But the range is significant nonetheless.

For example, at 3% annual average appreciation, TLCs are much greater after two years (from 14.7% to 18.4%) than they are after 22 years (from 5.3% to 9%).

Note also that no single plan is always the least expensive. After two years, the HUD plan is the least expensive at all appreciation rates. But from year seven on, the Freedom plan is almost always the least expensive.

On the other hand, the HomeFirst plan is the most expensive at every combination of appreciation rate and loan term in the table.

Lump Sum Leftovers

Table 32 shows how much equity would be left at various points in the future. It is based on a 75-year-old borrower living in a home worth $150,000. All the figures come from the leftover equity tables on the various plans that you saw in **Part TWO**.

Table 32 assumes that you take the full amount of cash available to you in a single lump sum at closing: $63,672 from the HECM plan, $46,000 from the Household plan, $37,483 from the HomeFirst plan, and $64,664 from the Freedom plan (see **Table 29**).

250

*Table 32: Leftover Equity on Lump Sums from Four
Reverse Mortgage Plans to a 75-Year-Old Living
in a $150,000 Home**

	at end of year	**Leftover Equity**			
		HUD/ HECM	**HOUSE HOLD**	**HOME- FIRST**	**FREE- DOM**
Average	2	$54,245	$74,485	$85,475	$50,812
Annual Home	7	2,032	19,025	39,597	27,000
Appreciation	12	0	0	0	27,000
= 0%	17	0	0	0	27,000
	22	0	0	0	27,000
Average	2	62,741	82,981	93,971	59,308
Annual Home	7	34,099	51,092	71,664	35,016
Appreciation	12	0	0	14,774	41,849
= 3%	17	0	0	0	49,768
	22	0	0	0	58,949
Average	2	71,487	91,727	102,717	68,054
Annual Home	7	72,288	89,281	109,853	44,564
Appreciation	12	60,218	57,458	96,581	62,300
= 6%	17	23,169	0	36,926	86,036
	22	0	0	0	117,798

The leftover equity amounts in this table come from the leftover equity
tables in **Part TWO**. They assume financing of all loan costs, and are
based on the interest rate assumptions discussed in **Chapter 22**.

In general, **Table 32** shows you that the more your home grows in value, the more equity you will have left in the future.

For example, if the value does not grow at all, you will be out of equity by the end of the twelfth year in three of the plans. But at 6% appreciation after 12 years, you retain anywhere from $57,458 to $96,581.

The HomeFirst plan always leaves you with the most equity through the seventh year. From year 12 on, the Freedom plan generally leaves you with the most equity.

The Freedom program always leaves at least 25% of your home's equity because it requires that you conserve at least that amount.

Summary Comparisons

Way back in **Chapter 3,** you learned to ask three basic questions about any reverse mortgage:

✓ What do you get?

✓ What do you pay?

✓ What would be left at the end of the loan?

Later on you learned that the answers to the second and third questions depend on how long you live in your home and what happens to its value.

*Table 33: Lump Sums, TLCs, and Leftover Equity
after **Twelve Years** at 3% Appreciation for a
75-Year-Old Living in a $150,000 Home*

	Lump Sum at Closing	TLC Rate	Leftover Equity
HUD/HECM	$63,672	9.5%	0
HOUSEHOLD	$46,000	12.3%	0
HOMEFIRST	$37,483	13.3%	$14,774
FREEDOM	$64,664	7.4%	$41,849

Table 33 answers the three basic questions for a 75-year-old borrower living in a $150,000 home, assuming 3% appreciation and a *twelve-year* term.

The life expectancy of a 75-year-old female is 11.6 years. For a 75-year-old male it's 8.9 years (see page 63). And keep in mind that not all reverse mortgage borrowers will live in their homes until death. Some will move - and repay their loans - sooner.

So **Table 34** shows TLC rates and leftover equity after *seven years*. Note in particular how much difference five years make when it comes to leftover equity - except for the Freedom plan.

Less Likely

The assumptions in **Table 33** and **34** (3% appreciation and 7 to 12 years) may be the most likely ones for a 75-year-old. But what about the less likely outcomes?

Table 34: Lump Sums, TLCs, and Leftover Equity
*after **Seven Years** at 3% Appreciation for a*
75-Year-Old Living in a $150,000 Home

	Lump Sum at Closing	TLC Rate	Leftover Equity
HUD/HECM	$63,672	11	$34,099
HOUSEHOLD	46,000	13.8	51,092
HOMEFIRST	37,483	14.1	71,664
FREEDOM	64,664	10.7	35,016

The figures in **Tables 33** and **34** are taken directly from **Tables 29**, **31**, and **32**. So if you want, you can put together similar tables for other appreciation rates and loan terms.

What would such a table look like at 3% appreciation at the end of two years? Or 22 years? At 6% appreciation? Or at 0%?

Making Your Own

If you are considering a specific reverse mortgage offer, you can put together tables like these using information from your lender.

Just make certain you get the TLC rate required by the Truth-in-Lending requirements of the Federal Reserve. And be sure to figure the leftover equity based on the projected total amount owed that is used to determine the TLC.

Chapter **24**

Comparing Creditlines

Are you looking for a creditline so that you can control the timing and amount of your cash advances?

This chapter compares the reverse mortgage plans that let you put all the money available to you into a creditline.

But first let's consider some of the basics.

Creditline Basics

A creditline makes your home equity available to you as you need it. That's very attractive, because it puts you in control.

But it also opens up some basic questions, such as

✓ What should you use it for?

✓ How should you use it? and

✓ When should you take out a creditline?

Creditline Uses

Chapter 23 warned you about investing or banking lump·sum advances. These warnings generally hold true for creditlines.

Chapter 23 also encouraged you to check out specific alternatives for paying off debts and for making home repairs or improvements. This advice holds true for creditlines advances as well.

Using a Creditline

A reverse mortgage creditline is something like a savings or checking account. But it also has some unique features. To use a creditline wisely, you need to understand that its familiar aspects and its unique aspects can contradict each other.

More Now, Less Later

The more credit you use now, the less you'll have later.

That's especially important if your home equity is your largest or your last remaining major asset. It means that once you use up a creditline, you may have nothing else to fall back on.

And if your loan balance has reached your nonrecourse limit, there may be no equity left if you decide to sell and move. So you've got to be careful how you use a creditline.

Less Now, More Costly

But you also can be "too careful" in using a creditline. For example, if you never use it, or if you hardly ever use it, or if you use it only for minor expenses, then it may be *extremely expensive.*

Think about it. If the amount of cash you actually get is small relative to the cost of setting up the loan, the TLC rate will be very high.

This doesn't mean you should be loose with your creditline to get a low TLC. But it does mean that you should only take out a creditline in the first place if you have a significant current need for it.

Closing a Creditline

If you don't need cash from a creditline at closing, or if you don't expect to use it much for the first year or so, then you shouldn't be taking out the loan.

At least not yet. Wait until you do have a real need for cash. That way your real cost will be lower.

And - if you wait to close the loan - you'll probably also be eligible for a larger creditline. After all, you'll be older, and your house probably will be worth more.

So don't get a creditline just to have one. Get it because you need it now. Otherwise wait until you do.

Creditline Benefits

Tables 35-36 compare the amounts you could get from the three private sector programs that offered a creditline program in the Fall of 1994.

These are the same amounts that you saw in Tables 29 and 30 in the last chapter. (If you take all the money out of your creditline at closing, that's the same as getting a lump sum.) So the lump sum benefit patterns discussed on pages 247-248 generally hold true for creditlines as well.

HUD Equity Limits

In particular, notice the effect of HUD's 203-b limits on the initial creditlines for homes worth $200,000 and $250,000. They aren't much different from the amounts for a $150,000 home because the highest 203-b limit is $152,363. And keep in mind that the limit in some rural areas is as low as $77,197.

*Table 35: Creditlines for **Single Borrowers** from Three Reverse Mortgage Plans*

HOME VALUE	AGE	HUD/ HECM	HOUSE- HOLD	HOME- FIRST
$150,000	65	$43,079*	$26,400	$19,583
	70	52,604*	33,100	27,788
	75	63,672*	46,000	37,483
	80	75,711*	57,000	48,155
	85	88,161*	78,000	58,392
	90	100,487*	92,300	68,562
$200,000	65	$43,864*	$35,400	$26,579
	70	53,537*	44,300	37,499
	75	64,778*	61,600	50,400
	80	77,003*	76,200	64,598
	85	89,645*	104,200	78,214
	90	102,158*	123,200	91,738
$250,000	65	$43,864*	$44,400	$33,576
	70	53,537*	55,600	47,210
	75	64,778*	77,100	63,317
	80	77,003*	95,400	81,040
	85	89,645*	130,400	98,036
	90	102,158*	154,200	114,915

.The creditlines in this table were available in the Fall of 1994. They assume financing of all loan costs, and are based on the interest rate assumptions discussed in **Chapter 22**.
*Assuming a 203-b limit of $152,363. Also, this creditline grows larger each month (see discussion on pages 261-262).

*Table 36: Creditlines for **Joint Borrowers** from Three Reverse Mortgage Plans*

HOME VALUE	AGE	HUD/ HECM	HOUSE- HOLD	HOME- FIRST
$150,000	65	$43,079*	$20,800	$19,583
	70	52,604*	26,400	27,788
	75	63,672*	37,000	37,483
	80	75,711*	46,000	48,155
	85	88,161*	63,300	58,392
	90	100,487*	78,000	68,562
$200,000	65	$43,864*	$28,000	$26,579
	70	53,537*	35,400	37,499
	75	64,778*	49,500	50,400
	80	77,003*	61,600	64,598
	85	89,645*	84,600	78,214
	90	102,158*	104,200	91,738
$250,000	65	$43,864*	$35,100	$33,576
	70	53,537*	44,400	47,210
	75	64,778*	62,100	63,317
	80	77,003*	77,000	81,040
	85	89,645*	105,900	98,036
	90	102,158*	130,400	114,915

The creditlines in this table were available in the Fall of 1994. They assume financing of all loan costs, and are based on the interest rate assumptions discussed in **Chapter 22**.
*Assuming a 203-b limit of $152,363. Also, this creditline grows larger each month (see discussion on pages 261-262).

HUD Creditline Growth

On the other hand, the HUD/HECM creditlines in **Tables 35-36** *grow larger over time.* On all current loans,* they grow by the "expected" rate plus 0.5%.

The expected rate assumed in the tables is 8.81%. So the *gross* creditline will grow by 9.31% per year.

If the rate charged on the loan balance turns out to be the expected rate (plus the 0.5% periodic insurance premium), then the remaining available *net* creditline will grow by 9.31%.

Growth versus No-Growth

Table 37 shows how important HUD's growing creditline can be over time. It is based on a 75-year-old borrower living in a $250,000 home. It assumes that the borrower takes out one-half of her available creditline at closing, and none after that.

This may not be a typical usage pattern. But it does illustrate the potential difference between a creditline that grows, and ones that do not. In general, the more you use a creditline closer to closing, the less important the growth factor will be.

---

*HUD is currently considering a proposal to change the manner in which its creditline grows. If it does change, it will only be on HECMs made after a certain date. The proposal is to have the creditline grow by the same rate as the one actually being charged on the loan balance at the time of the creditline increase, not the expected rate. This would eliminate the current possibility that after many years of net growth, an increased creditline could then decrease if the rate being charged is always greater than the expected rate.

Table 37: Remaining Creditline for a 75-Year-Old in a $250,000 Home Using One-Half at Closing

	HUD/ HECM	HOUSE- HOLD	HOME- FIRST
Available Creditline at Closing	$64,778	$77,100	$63,317
Creditline Used at Closing	$32,389	$38,550	$31,658
Remaining Creditline			
After 2 Years	$38,990	$38,550	$31,659
7 Years	61,992	38,550	31,659
12 Years	98,564	38,550	31,659
17 Years	156,712	38,550	31,659
22 Years	249,165	38,550	31,659

Creditline Costs

A creditline can be the least expensive or the most expensive type of reverse mortgage - depending on how you use it.

If you don't use it much, as discussed earlier, it can be extremely expensive. If you use it all at closing, on the other hand, it can be the least costly choice.

To compare the cost of different creditlines, therefore, you must assume the same usage pattern. **Table 38** is based on the assumption that you use one-half of the available creditline at closing, and no more.

Table 38: TLC Rates on Creditlines from Three Reverse Mortgage Plans to a 75-Year-Old Living in a $150,000 Home*

	at end of year	Total Loan Cost Rate		
		HUD/ HECM	HOUSE- HOLD	HOME- FIRST
Average	2	19.6%	22%	23.8%
Annual Home	7	12.6	15.1	15.5
Appreciation	12	11.4	14	14.1
= 0%	17	8.7	10.7	11.9
	22	6.7	8.2	9.2
Average	2	19.6%	22%	23.8%
Annual Home	7	12.6	15.1	15.5
Appreciation	12	11.4	14	14.1
= 3%	17	10.8	13.5	13.6
	22	9.7	11.2	12.1
Average	2	19.6%	22%	23.8%
Annual Home	7	12.6	15.1	15.5
Appreciation	12	11.4	14	14.1
= 6%	17	10.8	13.5	13.6
	22	10.5	13.3	13.3

*The TLC rates in this table come from the TLC tables in **Part TWO**. They assume financing of all loan costs, and are based on the interest rate assumptions discussed in **Chapter 22**.

Table 38 is based on a 75-year-old borrower living in a $150,000 home. Assuming a "half at closing" usage pattern, it shows that the HUD/HECM plan always has the lowest TLC rates, and the HomeFirst plan has the highest.

Creditline Leftovers

Table 39 compares the amount of leftover equity for a 75-year-old borrower living in a $150,000 home, based on creditline amounts from Table 35.

Table 39 assumes you take one-half the available creditline at closing, and nothing more until taking the rest just before loan maturity. The remaining available creditline is then included in the amount of leftover equity.

(Remember, however, that only a borrower can use a creditline. If you were to die before you could make the final withdrawal assumed in Table 39, your estate would not receive the asterisked amounts in that table. Instead, it would get a lesser amount, or maybe nothing at all.)

At 0% and at 3% appreciation, Table 39 shows that the HomeFirst plan leaves the most equity in the earlier years of the loan, and the HUD plan leaves the most in the later years.

At 6% appreciation, HomeFirst leaves the most at every point except if the loan ends after 22 years.

264

Table 39: Leftover Equity on Creditlines from Three
Reverse Mortgage Plans to a 75-Year-Old
Living in a $150,000 Home*

	at end of year	**Leftover Equity**		
		HUD/ HECM	HOUSE- HOLD	HOME- FIRST
Average	2	$92,569	$103,921	$109,483
Annual Home	7	62,966	73,571	84,399
Appreciation	12	96,881*	23,000*	38,352
= 0%	17	154,037*	23,000*	18,742*
	22	244,911*	23,000*	18,742*
Average	2	$101,065	$112,417	$117,979
Annual Home	7	95,033	105,638	116,466
Appreciation	12	96,881*	76,726	97,746
= 3%	17	154,037*	23,000*	44,897
	22	244,911*	23,000*	18,742*
Average	2	$109,811	$121,163	$126,725
Annual Home	7	133,222	143,827	154,655
Appreciation	12	157,100	158,533	179,553
= 6%	17	177,206	149,261	189,967
	22	244,911*	83,204	161,853

*Leftover equity equals home value minus total amount owed minus the cost of selling the home, which is assumed to be 7% of the home's value. *Leftover equity also includes remaining creditline assumed to be withdrawn just prior to loan maturity.*

Summary Comparisons

For a 75-year-old borrower living in a $150,000 home, **Tables 40** and **41** summarize

✓ the benefits,

✓ the cost, and

✓ the leftover equity

after twelve years and after seven years, assuming 3% annual average home appreciation.

The assumptions in these tables are the most probable ones for a 75-year-old. At that age, your life expectancy ranges from 11.6 years for females to 8.9 years for males. And some borrowers will pay back their loans even sooner.

*Table 40: Creditlines, TLCs, and Leftover Equity after **Twelve Years** at 3% Appreciation for a 75-Year-Old Living in a $150,000 Home*

	Initial Creditline	TLC Rate	Leftover Equity
HUD/HECM	$63,672	11.4%	$96,881
HOUSEHOLD	$46,000	14%	$76,726
HOMEFIRST	$37,483	14.1%	$97,746

*Table 41: Creditlines, TLCs, and Leftover Equity after **Seven Years** at 3% Appreciation for a 75-Year-Old Living in a $150,000 Home*

	Initial Creditline	TLC Rate	Leftover Equity
HUD/HECM	$63,672	12.6%	$95,033
HOUSEHOLD	$46,000	15.1%	$105,638
HOMEFIRST	$37,483	15.5%	$116,466

The figures in these tables are taken from **Tables 35, 38,** and **39.** So if you're curious, go ahead and use those table to put together any other summary comparisons that interest you.

Monthly Up Next

Creditline and lump sum comparisons are similar in many respects. A lump sum, after all, is just a creditline that's all used up at closing.

But the comparisons of monthly advances in the next chapter involve an added wrinkle: annuities.

Chapter 25

Comparing Monthly Plans

Are you looking for a monthly cash advance?

This chapter compares the reverse mortgages that will send you a fixed cash advance every month.

The comparisons assume that you take a monthly advance only - without a lump sum at closing or a creditline in addition to the monthly advance.

In fact, you probably do have some immediate lump sum need or would want a creditline for irregular or unexpected expenses. But by assuming monthly advances only, you will be better able to compare the benefits and costs of the monthly advances.

Monthly Benefits

You can get fixed monthly cash advances for

✓ a fixed period of time ("term" advances),

✓ as long as you live in your home ("tenure" advances), or

✓ the rest of your life ("lifetime" advances).

Of the programs that offer monthly advances, only the Household and HomeFirst plans do not offer term advances. Only the HUD plan offers tenure advances, and only the HomeFirst and Freedom plans offer lifetime advances.

Term Advances

In general, the shorter the term of advances, the greater the advances will be. *But term advances stop at the end of the term, and some of these loans must be repaid when the advances stop (see **Chapter 17**).*

So unless you intend to sell and move, or unless your doctor says you are unlikely to outlive your monthly advances, or unless you otherwise expect your need for monthly income will stop, you are probably going to prefer tenure or lifetime advances.

You will most likely get less cash each month that way. But you will certainly get greater security.

270

Open-Ended Advances

When you choose tenure or lifetime advances, you get an open-ended guarantee that your monthly cash advances will continue for an indefinite period of time.

Tables 42-43 show how much you could get from the programs that provide open-ended advances. They assume financing of all costs, and the interest rates discussed in **Chapter 22**.

HUD Limits

The HUD advances in the tables assume that the 203-b limit in your area is $152,363. If it is less, then the HUD advances will be less than the tables show. The lowest 203-b limit is $77,197.

Even assuming the largest 203-b limit, however, the HUD plan generally provides smaller advances on homes valued at $200,000 and above.

Annuity Taxation

On the other hand, you must take into account the overall tax implications of the annuity advances provided by the HomeFirst and Freedom plans. These issues were discussed in **Chapter 22**.

Tenure versus Lifetime

Also keep in mind that the HUD plan provides *tenure* advances, while the HomeFirst and Freedom plans provide *lifetime* advances. The difference may or may not end up being an important one.

*Table 42: Monthly Advances for **Single Borrowers**
from Three Reverse Mortgage Plans*

HOME VALUE	AGE	HUD/ HECM	HOME- FIRST	FREE- DOM
$150,000	65	$345*	$261**	$372**
	70	432*	369**	487**
	75	544*	536**	647**
	80	691*	697**	873**
	85	904*	941**	1,163**
	90	1,280*	1,337**	1,517**
$200,000	65	$351*	$350**	$498**
	70	439*	494**	651**
	75	553*	717**	864**
	80	703*	931**	1,167**
	85	919*	1,258**	1,554**
	90	1,301*	1,787**	2,026**
$250,000	65	$351*	$439**	$623**
	70	439*	619**	815**
	75	553*	898**	1,083**
	80	703*	1,166**	1,461**
	85	919*	1,574**	1,944**
	90	1,301*	2,236**	2,536**

The amounts in this table were available in the Fall of 1994, assuming
financing of all costs, and interest rates discussed in **Chapter 22**.
*__Tenure advances__, assuming a 203-b limit of $152,363.
**__Lifetime advances__, assuming annuities with no "period certain."

272

*Table 43: Monthly Advances for **Joint Borrowers**
from Three Reverse Mortgage Plans*

HOME VALUE	AGE	HUD/ HECM	HOME- FIRST	FREE- DOM
$150,000	65	$345*	$248**	$258***
	70	432*	345**	336***
	75	544*	486**	443***
	80	691*	624**	596***
	85	904*	825**	810**
	90	1,280*	1,079**	1,099**
$200,000	65	$351*	$333**	$345***
	70	439*	462**	449***
	75	553*	651**	593***
	80	703*	834**	796***
	85	919*	1,103**	1,083**
	90	1,301*	1,442**	1,469**
$250,000	65	$351*	$418**	$432***
	70	439*	579**	563***
	75	553*	815**	742***
	80	703*	1,044**	997***
	85	919*	1,380**	1,356**
	90	1,301*	1,804**	1,837**

These amounts were available in the Fall of 1994, assuming financing of all costs, and interest rates discussed in **Chapter 22**.
***Tenure advances**, assuming a 203-b limit of $152,363.
****Lifetime advances**, assuming annuities with no "period certain" except ***, where annuities include a 4-year period certain.

If you live in your home for the rest of your life, you would not get any extra advances from a lifetime program. But if you sell and move, you would get extra advances from a lifetime plan. And that may or may not be to your advantage.

Much would depend on why you would sell and move, and how much equity you would have left after paying off the loan (in addition to any continuing annuity advances).

Moving Where?

For example, if you move into a nursing home or assisted living facility, you might prefer having more cash in the form of leftover equity rather than in the form of a continuing annuity advance.

This might mean the difference between entering a nursing home as a private paying resident versus a Medicaid-financed resident. It might also make it possible for you to cover the entrance fee for an assisted living facility.

And it's likely that most of your continuing monthly advance would go to pay ongoing residency costs in either case.

Elsewhere?

If you move for other reasons, the comparison of tenure versus lifetime advances may depend somewhat less on the form of your leftover cash.

But it will depend on the total amount of leftover cash, which will be discussed later in this chapter.

274

Monthly Costs

Table 44 shows Total Loan Cost (TLC) rates for a 75-year-old borrower living in a $150,000 home. It assumes the borrower puts all available funds into a monthly advance.

According to the table, the HUD/HECM plan has the lowest TLCs after two years and after seven years at all appreciation rates. At the end of year 12 and later, the Freedom plan generally has the lowest TLC rates.

On the other hand, the Freedom plan has by far the highest TLC rates at the end of two years. By the end of year seven and later, the HomeFirst plan always has the highest TLCs.

Keep in mind, however, that TLCs simply project the real cost of the money you receive to a given point in time. They do not take into account the amount of leftover equity at that time, whether it's in the form of a continuing monthly annuity advances or net sale proceeds left over after repaying the loan.

Monthly Leftovers

Table 45 shows how much equity would be left for a 75-year-old borrower living in a $150,000 home. *The figures do not include the value of the continuing monthly annuity advances in the HomeFirst plan ($536) and in the Freedom plan ($647).*

Table 44: TLC Rates on Monthly Advances from Three Reverse Mortgage Plans to a 75-Year-Old Living in a $150,000 Home*

		Total Loan Cost Rate		
	at end of year	HUD/ HECM	HOME- FIRST	FREE- DOM
Average	2	51.5%	88.2%	146.7%
Annual Home	7	14.7	19.6	18.7
Appreciation	12	8.8	9	3
= 0%	17	2.6	2.7	-1.9
	22	-0.3	-0.1	-4.1
Average	2	51.5%	98.6%	146.7%
Annual Home	7	14.7	23.6	23.2
Appreciation	12	11.7	13.9	8
= 3%	17	7.8	7.9	3.5
	22	5.2	5.3	1.8
Average	2	51.5%	107.8%	146.7%
Annual Home	7	14.7	27.4	27.6
Appreciation	12	11.7	17.5	12.6
= 6%	17	10.7	12.4	8.3
	22	9.7	9.8	6.6

*The TLC rates in this table come from the TLC tables in **Part TWO**. They assume financing of all costs, and are based on the interest rate assumptions discussed in **Chapter 22**.

*Table 45: Leftover Equity on Monthly Advances
from Three Reverse Mortgage Plans to a
75-Year-Old Living in a $150,000 Home*

| | at end of year | Leftover Equity* | | |
		HUD/ HECM	HOME- FIRST	FREE -DOM
Average	2	$116,500	$104,362*	$50,812*
Annual	7	59,352	42,649*	27,000*
Home	12	0	0*	27,000*
Appreciation	17	0	0*	27,000*
= 0%	22	0	0*	27,000*
Average	2	$124,996	$108,107*	$59,308*
Annual	7	91,419	56,785*	35,016*
Home	12	27,882	0*	41,849*
Appreciation	17	0	0*	49,768*
= 3%	22	0	0*	58,949*
Average	2	$133,742	$111,963*	$68,054*
Annual	7	129,608	73,621*	44,564*
Home	12	109,689	18,888*	62,300*
Appreciation	17	60,161	0*	86,036*
= 6%	22	0	0*	117,798*

All figures are taken from leftover equity tables in **Part TWO**, assuming financing of all costs, and interest rates discussed in **Chapter 22**.
*Does not include continuing monthly advance from annuity ($536 from HomeFirst; $647 from Freedom).

Of course if the loan ends due to your death, there are no continuing monthly annuity advances unless

✓ you have a surviving joint borrower, or

✓ in the Freedom plan, your surviving joint borrower and you were 85 years of age or less at the time of loan closing and you both die within four years of closing.

Valuing the Annuity

On the other hand, if the loan ends because you decide to sell and move, you would continue to receive monthly annuity advances from the HomeFirst and Freedom plans for the rest of your life - no matter where you live.

The financial value of these annuity advances can be estimated. The simplest way to do it is to figure out how much money you would need in a savings account to be able to take out the same amount you could get from an annuity for the rest of your life.

For example, assume you are a 75-year old single female living in a $150,000 home who signs up for the Freedom plan. Now assume that you decide to sell and move 7 years later.

At age 82, your life expectancy is about 7.7 years. So the question is, "How much money would you need in savings at that point to let you withdraw $647 each month for the next 7.7 years?" Assuming an interest rate of 5%, the answer is $49,482.

With Adjustments

This simple method both understates and overstates the value of the annuity.

It understates the value because an annuity keeps paying for as long as you live. So if you live *beyond* your life expectancy - as many people do - then you would continue getting $647 each month from the Freedom annuity for as long as you live. In other words, you would get *more* than the estimated value of $49,482.

In fact, for the savings account to be more closely comparable to the annuity, you would need more than $49,482 to provide the kind of income *security* that an annuity gives you. If you wanted coverage for 150% of your life expectancy, for example, you would need about $67,911.

On the other hand, if it turns out that you do not make it to your life expectancy, you would only get monthly advances for as long as you live. So you would actually get *less* than the estimated $49,482.

In addition, the tax considerations discussed in **Chapter 22** might make the real worth of Freedom's monthly annuity less than its $647 face value.

Including the Annuity

Table 46 is the same as **Table 45** except that it includes the estimated value of the HomeFirst and Freedom annuities, using the simple method discussed above. These comparisons assume that you sell and move, and then live to your life expectancy.

Part THREE: Nest Egg Comparisons

*Table 46: Leftover Equity **Including Estimated Annuity Value** from Three Reverse Mortgage Plans to a 75-Year-Old Living in a $150,000 Home**

	at end of year	HUD/ HECM	HOME- FIRST	FREE -DOM
		Leftover Equity*		
Average	2	$116,500	$156,228*	$113,419*
Annual	7	59,352	83,642*	76,482*
Home	12	0	31,383*	64,882*
Appreciation	17	0	23,791*	55,718*
= 0%	22	0	18,848*	49,751*
Average	2	$124,996	$159,973*	$121,915*
Annual	7	91,419	97,778*	84,498*
Home	12	27,882	31,383*	79,731*
Appreciation	17	0	23,791*	78,486*
= 3%	22	0	18,848*	81,700*
Average	2	$133,742	$163,829*	$130,661*
Annual	7	129,608	114,614*	94,046*
Home	12	109,689	50,271*	100,182*
Appreciation	17	60,161	23,791*	114,754*
= 6%	22	0	18,848*	140,549*

*Figures are taken from leftover equity tables in **Part TWO,** assuming financing of all costs, and interest rates discussed in **Chapter 22.**
*Includes estimated value of continuing monthly advance from annuity ($536 from HomeFirst; $647 from Freedom).

280

When the value of the annuity is included, the HomeFirst plan generally leaves the most total cash after two years and after seven years. From the end of the twelfth year and thereafter, the Freedom plan generally leaves the most total cash.

Summary Comparisons

Tables 47-48 summarize the monthly benefits, total cost, and leftover equity for a 75-year-old borrower living in a $150,000 home after twelve years and after seven years, assuming 3% annual average appreciation.

Both tables show leftover equity under two assumptions. "Without equity" shows the net sale proceeds that would be left after paying off your loan. In other words, it is the amount that would be left for your heirs if you died after seven or twelve years.

"With annuity" shows that total plus the estimated value of the continuing annuities in the HomeFirst and Freedom plans. The figures are taken from **Table 46**.

For 75-year-olds, life expectancy ranges from 11.6 years for females to 8.9 years for males. Also keep in mind that some borrowers will pay back their loans even sooner.

If you're interested in other combinations of loan terms and appreciation rates, you can use the figures from **Tables 42, 44-46** to make your own summary comparisons.

*Table 47: Monthly Advances, TLCs, and Leftover Equity
after **Twelve Years** at 3% Appreciation for a
75-Year-Old Living in a $150,000 Home*

			Leftover Equity	
	MONTHLY ADVANCE	TLC Rate	Without Annuity	With Annuity
HUD/HECM	$544 (tenure)	11.7	$27,882	$27,882
HOMEFIRST	$536 (life)	13.9	0	$31,383
FREEDOM	$647 (life)	8	$41,849	$79,731

*Table 48: Monthly Advances, TLCs, and Leftover Equity
after **Seven Years** at 3% Appreciation for a
75-Year-Old Living in a $150,000 Home*

			Leftover Equity	
	MONTHLY ADVANCE	TLC Rate	Without Annuity	With Annuity
HUD/HECM	$544 (tenure)	14.7	$91,419	$91,419
HOMEFIRST	$536 (life)	23.6	$56,785	$97,778
FREEDOM	$647 (life)	23.2	$35,016	$84,498

Mondo Combo

Now that you've compared each type of cash advance in isolation, it's time for the wonderful world of combinations.

Chapter 26

Comparing Combinations

In the last three chapters, you have seen a variety of reverse mortgage comparisons. But in each chapter, we assumed that you took all your available funds as just one of the basic types of cash advances.

This showed you how each plan compares with the others in providing the different types of cash advances one at a time.

But it also showed you a lot about comparing combinations of cash advances types. Any combination, after all, is made up of the different parts you've just analyzed and compared in detail.

Lump + Line

One of the most flexible combinations is a lump sum at closing plus a creditline. This allows you to take care of some immediate needs and have a ready reserve for the future.

In fact, as discussed in **Chapter 24**, you really shouldn't be thinking about taking out a creditline unless you do have some immediate reason for doing so.

In the plans that provide lump sums and creditlines, you can split your available funds between the two in any way you choose. The benefits tables in **Chapters 23** and **24** show you how much you can get from each plan.

In comparing the creditline part of the combination, you need to keep in mind that the HUD/HECM creditline grows over time (see pages 261-262).

Lump versus Line

If you live in a higher-valued home and expect to take a significant lump sum at closing, you also should consider a plan that does not even have a creditline.

As discussed in **Chapter 23**, putting a lump sum advance in the bank is generally an inferior alternative to a creditline. The interest you pay on the full amount of the lump sum advance is greater than any interest you can safely earn on the lump sum deposit.

So to the extent that a deposited lump sum is not used, you are incurring unnecessary costs.

But a lump sum *might* be a reasonable option

✓ if the lump sum is much greater than any creditline alternative,

✓ if you have immediate needs for much or all of the creditline, and

✓ if the cost of the lump sum is determined by a "percent of value" formula in any case.

Depends on Usage

For example, the Freedom plan provides a lump sum of $108,161 to a 75-year-old borrower living in a $250,000 home. The comparable creditlines from other plans range from $63,317 to $77,100.

Assume that your immediate needs would use up most or all of the creditlines. If you take the Freedom lump sum instead, you would have much more cash available after meeting those needs.

But if your immediate needs require very little of the Freedom lump sum and you use little thereafter, the real cost of the money you use could be extremely high. Remember, this plan is based on "percent of value" pricing. So the total cost is the same no matter how much of the lump sum you actually use. The less you use, the greater the effective cost to you.

Growth versus Interest

If your immediate needs use up about half the creditline, then the lump sum comparison also would have to take into account the growth of the HUD creditline.

Table 49 shows the remaining cash in a HUD creditline or a deposited Freedom lump sum for a 75-year-old borrower living in a $200,000 home.

In the HUD example, the borrower uses one-half the available HUD creditline ($32,389) at closing and none after that. The remaining gross creditline of $32,389 then grows at 9.31% per year.

In the Freedom example, the borrower uses $32,389 from the available lump sum of $86,412 at closing. The remaining $54,023 is deposited in a secure account at 5% interest and never withdrawn.

As you can see, the total cash remaining available to the borrower in this example is greater under the Freedom plan until nearly the end of the 12th year.

Draws versus Withdrawals

If the borrower uses some of the remaining cash after closing, it would reduce the creditline by more than it would reduce the deposited lump sum.

Draws on the HUD creditline *plus all the interest that accrues on such draws in the future* is subtracted from the gross remaining creditline. By contrast, only the principal withdrawals are subtracted from the deposited Freedom lump sum account.

286

Table 49: Remaining Cash Available to a 75-Year-Old Borrower Living in a $200,000 Home

	HUD/HECM CREDITLINE	FREEDOM LUMP SUM
Cash Available at Closing	$64,778	$86,412
Cash Used at Closing	$32,389	$32,389
Remaining Cash Available to Borrower		
At Closing	$32,389*	$54,023**
After 2 Years	38,990*	59,692**
7 Years	61,992*	76,607**
12 Years	98,564*	98,314**
17 Years	156,712*	126,172**
22 Years	249,165*	161,924**

*Assuming net creditline grows at 9.31% per year; future creditline draws *plus interest* would be subtracted from the remaining creditline.
**Assuming lump sum is deposited in an account at 5% interest; future withdrawals of *principal only* would be subtracted from the account.

So if the borrower took an additional $30,000 at the end of seven years, for example, the net remaining HUD creditline at that time would be $31,992. But from that point forward, the rising amount of interest on the $30,000 draw *also* would be subtracted from the gross creditline amount. If the rate charged was 9.31%, for example, that would be $17,699 in interest over the next five years. So the remaining net creditline at the end of 12 years would be $50,865.

By contrast, a $30,000 withdrawal at the same time from the deposited Freedom lump sum would reduce that account to $46,607. Five years later, this new balance would have earned $13,207 in interest at 5%. So the remaining cash after 12 years would be $59,814.

If the borrower does not take the additional $30,000 after seven years, the remaining cash in the Freedom plan's lump sum account after 12 years is *$250 less* than the remaining HUD creditline.

But if the borrower does take the additional $30,000 after seven years, the Freedom plans leaves *$8,949 more* than the HUD plan after 12 years.

So you not only have to figure that the accounts grow at different rates. You also have to keep in mind that *HUD creditline draws reduce the net creditline by more than withdrawals from a deposited lump sum do.*

Pre-Tax versus Post-Tax

A deposited lump sum gives you money in the bank. It's in your name and it's earning interest. But that can lead to taxation.

At moderate to upper income levels, the interest you earn may be taxable. At lower income levels, the amount in a savings account may make you ineligible for government programs. Medicaid rules, for example, permit only very small amounts of resources.

A creditline, by contrast, does not earn interest. And the money in it is generally not counted as a resource unless and until you actually take it out.

288

Comparing Costs

Comparing the cost of a creditline to the cost of a deposited lump sum is tricky.

In calculating TLC rates, the usage pattern is key. If a creditline is used a lot and early, the TLCs are much lower than if it is used little and late.

With a deposited lump sum, the TLC calculation is based on the fact that you receive all the money on the first day. It does not take into account that you might bank some of it and use it like a creditline.

The result is that even though you might use a deposited lump sum in exactly the same way as you would a creditline, the TLC would be different. So it doesn't really work to compare the TLCs for one type of cash advance (or usage pattern) to another.

Alternative Costing

An alternative would be to change the TLC rate calculation by only counting the lump sum funds you use at closing or withdraw from the interest-bearing account. But that's getting a bit murky.

A more direct way is to assume identical usage patterns, and then compare the total of remaining cash and/or leftover equity.

Table 50 assumes that a 75-year-old in a $200,000 home uses half the available HUD creditline ($32,389) at closing and none after that. It then shows how much total cash would be left in the creditline or in leftover equity - whichever is greater.

*Table 50: Total Remaining Cash and/or Leftover Equity
for a 75-Year-Old in a $200,000 Home
at 3% Annual Average Appreciation*

	HUD/HECM CREDITLINE	FREEDOM LUMP SUM
Cash Available at Closing	$64,778	$86,412
Cash Used at Closing	$32,389	$32,389
Remaining Cash Available to Borrower at Closing	$32,389	$54,023
Total Remaining Cash and/or Leftover Equity		
After 2 Years	149,673*	138,768**
7 Years	151,074*	123,297**
12 Years	139,765*	154,112**
17 Years	156,712*	192,530**
22 Years	249,165*	240,523**

*Equals the remaining creditline growing at 9.31% OR the leftover
equity (which includes the remaining creditline), whichever is greater.
**Equals the leftover equity PLUS a $54,023 lump sum deposited in an
account earning 5% interest.

(A "whichever greater" method is used in the HUD
example because the leftover equity amount *includes*
the remaining creditline that the borrower is assumed
to draw just before repaying the loan. So adding the
two figures together would be double counting.)

Table 50 also assumes the borrower uses $32,389 from the Freedom lump sum of $86,412 at closing, and deposits the remaining $54,023 in a secure account at 5% interest.

The table shows what the balance in that account would grow to become plus the equity leftover after paying back the loan at various future times.

The HUD amounts are greater than the Freedom amounts at the end of years 2, 7, and 22. The Freedom amounts are greater than the HUD amounts at the end of years 12 and 17.

With Adjustments

The figures in **Table 50** assume no future draws from the creditline or withdrawals from the deposited lump sum. If you took the same additional cash from each after closing, the remaining Freedom amounts would be reduced by less than the remaining HUD amounts.

This would happen because - as discussed earlier - HUD draws reduce gross creditlines by principal plus interest. Withdrawals from a deposited lump sum, by contrast, reduce the balance by principal only.

So if you were to continue using the creditline and deposited lump sum after closing, the total remaining cash would decrease by less in the Freedom plan.

Whichever plan has the most remaining total cash in this comparison is the least expensive. That's what happens when you assume identical benefits. The plan with the most left over has a lower total cost.

Monthly Plus

All the other possible combinations of cash advance types include a monthly advance.

In the multi-purpose plans providing monthly advances, you can split your available funds between monthly advances and a lump sum and/or a creditline.

The HECM and HomeFirst plans have all three types of cash advances. The Freedom plan has a lump sum and a monthly advance - although in some cases a deposited lump sum can be a reasonable alternative to a creditline, as discussed in the previous eight pages.

The HECM and Freedom plans let you split up your available funds in any way you choose. There are no minimums or maximums. In the HomeFirst plan, by contrast, you must take a monthly advance of at least $150.

Comparing Benefits

Table 51 shows how much a 75-year-old borrower could get combining lump sum and monthly advances.

The table uses different monthly advances for homes of different value. But at each home value it uses the same monthly advance for each plan. This lets you see how much the lump sum would differ if the monthly advance is kept the same.

In all cases, the Freedom plan provides the largest lump sum in addition to the fixed monthly advance.

Table 51: Combinations of Lump Sum and Monthly Advances for a 75-Year-Old Borrower from Three Reverse Mortgage Programs*

		+ Lump Sum		
		HUD/ HECM	HOME- FIRST	FREE- DOM
HOME VALUE	MONTHLY ADVANCE			
$150,000	$300**	$28,539	$22,952	$31,587
$200,000	$400**	$17,934	$30,802	$42,472
$250,000	$500**	$6,223	$38,653	$53,405

*This table assumes that all costs are financed with the loan and is based on the closing cost and interest rate assumptions discussed in **Chapter 22.**
**The monthly advance from the HUD plan continues for as long as you live in your home. The monthly advance from the HomeFirst and Freedom plans continues for the rest of your life no matter where you live.

You also can combine a creditline with a monthly advance in the HECM and HomeFirst plans. If you used the same monthly advances as in **Table 51**, the creditline amounts would be the same as the lump sums in the HECM plan. In the HomeFirst plan, the creditlines would be $17,477 on the $150,000 home, $23,456 on the $200,000 home, and $29,434 on the $250,000 home.

Summary Comparisons

Tables 52-53 summarize the benefits, cost, and leftover equity for a 75-year-old borrower living in a $150,000 home who takes a $300 monthly advance plus a lump sum from three reverse mortgage plans.

Table 52 shows the TLC rates and leftover equity after twelve years; **Table 53** after seven years. Both tables assume an annual average home appreciation rate of 3%.

*Table 52: Combined Advances, TLCs, and Leftover
Equity after **Twelve Years** at 3% Appreciation
for a 75-Year-Old in a $150,000 Home*

	MONTHLY ADVANCE	LUMP SUM	TLC Rate	Leftover Equity
HUD/HECM	$300	$28,539	10.8%	$5,709
HOMEFIRST	$300	$22,952	12.3%	0
FREEDOM	$300	$31,587	8.2%	$41,849

*Table 53: Combined Advances, TLCs, and Leftover
Equity after **Seven Years** at 3% Appreciation
for a 75-Year-Old in a $150,000 Home*

	MONTHLY ADVANCE	LUMP SUM	TLC Rate	Leftover Equity
HUD/HECM	$300	$28,539	12.1%	$65,728
HOMEFIRST	$300	$22,952	16.8%	$49,363
FREEDOM	$300	$31,587	15.3%	$35,016

The leftover equity figures in **Tables 52-53** do not include the value of continuing annuity advances in the HomeFirst and Freedom plans. Using the valuation method described in **Chapter 25**, the value after seven years would be about $22,944, and after twelve years about $17,565.

But remember, annuities only have continuing value if you sell and move. And then much depends on what your needs are at that time.

Other Comparisons

Tables 52-53 show you the kind of comparisons that summarize the basic financial characteristics of reverse mortgages.

These types of comparisons can be put together for any specific loans with similar combinations of loan advances. Your lender can supply you with the basic information you need.

And if you are comparing two or more plans providing the same combination of advances, you can ask each lender to critique the information you get from the others. This process will help you develop a true "apples to apples" comparison.

Chapter 27

Being Careful

You wouldn't have made it to the last chapter of this book if you weren't a careful consumer.

And now that you've made it this far, you really understand that reverse mortgages present new types of opportunities and risks.

So let's wind things up with some explicit cautions. You now know what to look for, and most of what to look out for. Here's the rest of the "look out for's."

Sheep's Clothing

It's too bad - but perhaps inevitable - that a new product designed to let people help themselves would attract predators bent on helping *themselves* to other people's money.

You'll no doubt recognize them if you see them, no matter what they're wearing. So far, they've come in two basic varieties: "counselors" and "tinmen."

"Counselors"

What would you think of a reverse mortgage "counselor" who gets paid by a lender, but only if you take out a reverse mortgage? Sound more like a salesperson?

Or what about a "counselor" who's paid different amounts depending on which type of reverse mortgage you take out? Think the "recommendations" you'd get would be unbiased, with only your interests in mind?

After reading this book, you're no doubt better informed than any "counselor" you might meet. And a lot more trustworthy!

Legitimate counselors work for HUD-certified counseling agencies and have attended training sessions on reverse mortgages. They can be especially helpful in finding other programs for which you may be eligible. They get paid for counseling, period. Any HECM lender can refer you to these agencies.

"Tinmen"

No, not the kind in the "Wizard of Oz." The kind in the movie "Tinmen," about aluminum siding salesmen in Baltimore.

Guys who would sell it to you if you need it or not. Guys who might especially relish selling it to you if you *don't* need it.

Be careful of anyone who recommends a reverse mortgage who *also* has some idea about how you might spend the money it provides. Especially if they happen to benefit if you spend the money in the way they suggest.

These "tinmen" can be siding salespeople, home repair contractors, stockbrokers, or any number of others who are *primarily* looking to sell you something.

They might even be people you know and trust who think they need your money more than you do. Or people who have your interests in mind but who have little financial sense.

Whoever they happen to be, keep your distance.

Refinancing Alert

After you've taken out a reverse mortgage is no time to let your guard down. Maybe *this* is when the "tinmen" will arrive Or when you'll be offered a "fabulous deal" to refinance or extend your loan.

299

Be especially careful in considering any offer that looks "too good to pass up." There's a very good chance that it isn't.

Devilish Details

The devil is in the details. So be sure to compare the features of your current reverse mortgage with any proposed new reverse mortgage in detail.

You may get extra money from the new loan. But what will it really cost you? Is the extra money you get worth the added cost? Ask the lender to show you the total dollar amount you would owe at various points in the future under each loan. Ask for a TLC comparison. Get it in writing. Have the lender sign it.

Do both loans have the same itemized costs? Look at the interest rate details. Are you being switched from one interest rate index to another? Or is the "margin" the lender adds to the interest index being increased?

In short, be very cautious about any offer that comes your way to refinance or otherwise extend your reverse mortgage.

However

On the other hand, if your home appreciates rapidly over several years and interest rates decline sharply, it just might be worth investigating the matter on your own. Just remember, you'd need a lot of appreciation and much lower rates to make it worth your while.

Taxman Cometh?

When you take out a reverse mortgage, selling and moving is probably the furthest thing from your mind.

But many years later, you may consider changing your mind. If you do, you need to understand the tax consequences of selling a home. In fact, you should be generally aware of the potential outcomes even before you close a reverse mortgage loan.

As you learned in **Chapter 22,** if you sell after closing a reverse mortgage, it is possible that you could owe a capital gains (or alternative minimum) tax that is greater than your offsetting interest deductions.

And, in some of these cases, the net tax due could even be greater than the leftover equity you would get after paying off the loan.

Assessing the Possibility

In general, the possibility of net tax due appears to be greatest if, at closing,

✓ you intend to sell your home and move at some point in the future;

✓ you have already used the one-time capital gains exclusion, or if

✓ your potential gain already exceeds or is within range of $125,000;

✓ you intend to spend all the money you can possibly get from your reverse mortgage;

✓ you are in your sixties or early seventies (so your life expectancy is longer, and there may be more time during which additional gain could occur);

✓ you live in a high-valued home (so even small rates of appreciation can generate significant additional gain);

✓ you are single (so there will be no future "step-up in basis" at the death of a spouse);

✓ you are using none of the loan to refinance a first mortgage, and intend to use none of it to make substantial home improvements.

The more you can see yourself in this checklist, the greater the possibility is that you *might* have some amount of net tax due *if* you decide to sell your home *after* taking out a reverse mortgage.

Planning

Reverse mortgage lenders can project the interest you would owe - and the leftover equity you would have - at a future time. IRS publications can then help you estimate your potential capital gains (or alternative minimum) tax liabilities. And you can always seek advice from tax professionals.

You can plan to cover any projected net tax due (after interest deductions) with leftover cash from your reverse mortgage. For example, you can set aside funds in a creditline or use an equity conservation feature to safeguard the funds you might need.

You? Incapable?

None of us likes to think about it. But any of us can lose our ability to handle our own affairs. And the odds of that happening increase with age.

If it happens to you and you live by yourself, you might fail to meet your obligations under the loan agreement. For example, paying your property taxes and insurance, and keeping your home from falling into serious disrepair. And this could lead to default and foreclosure.

Or, *you might lose a lot of money* by failing to use a substantial creditline. This could happen if your remaining creditline is larger than the difference between your loan balance and your loan's nonrecourse limit. If you were to move or die before using the remaining creditline, you or your heirs would be left with the smaller amount.

So especially if you are frail or chronically ill, you should give some thought to preparing a "durable power of attorney" for financial and real state matters, and a "health care power of attorney" for medical treatment and home care services.

Your Creditline

Even if you don't become incapacitated, you could still misuse a creditline by failing to draw it all down toward the end of the loan.

Remember, your remaining creditline may at some point be greater than the amount of leftover equity you or your heirs would get if the loan were to be repaid. If this happens, you must be certain to take all the funds remaining in your creditline just before the end of the loan. If you fail to do this, you may be left with a much smaller amount of leftover cash.

Even if your remaining creditline is less than your leftover equity, you might still want to draw it all out before selling. Having the funds in hand sooner might make it easier for you to relocate.

Or, you might want to make a bequest more readily accessible to your heirs by placing the funds in a savings or money market account. Some borrowers have even used their creditlines to make an "early bequest" during their lifetimes.

Your Heirs

To avoid problems in settling your estate, your executor will need to know that there is a reverse mortgage on your home. If your will does not alert your heirs to this fact, the result could be significant confusion and cost.

For example, it may not be clear that the interest clock is ticking, or that shared appreciation costs may be growing, or that "percent of value" pricing may be reducing the estate prior to sale of the home.

Knowing the details of the reverse mortgage will help your executor make decisions about selling the home and repaying the loan. It also will make it easier for that person to explain the estate implications of the reverse mortgage to your heirs - if you have not already done so.

Your Self

In the end, however, the most important thing to look out for is yourself. After all, you are the person who will decide if, when, and how to use your new retirement nest egg.

If these decisions are made without accurate information or deliberative care, they can be a big mistake. But now that you've waded through this book, you are well prepared to make them.

And that's not all.

Your Help

You are now one of the few people in America who knows quite a bit about reverse mortgages. So, believe it or not, you are now a national resource that could be of significant help to others.

That might sound strange. In one sense, all you've done is read a book. But it's true. You *are* one of the few people nationwide who have taken the time to become educated about the new opportunities and risks of reverse mortgages.

You now know more about this topic than over 99% of the American people know. So you *are* in a position to educate and inform others in important ways.

Volunteer Counseling

You could be a big help to homeowners who might find this book tough going, for example. Or who might like to talk with a knowledgeable person about their specific situations.

There's a movement afoot to train and deploy a corps of volunteer reverse mortgage counselors. If it spreads to your area, you may have an opportunity to put your new knowledge to work in a good cause.

Would you like to be contacted if a volunteer counseling program develops in your area? If you would, send a *postcard* with your name and address to NCHEC Counseling, 7373 147th Street, Apple Valley, MN 55124.

Eyes and Ears

You also could be a big help to me and to others who are monitoring the development of this market from a consumer standpoint. The best way for us to learn about actual lending practices and consumer interests is through direct contact with consumers.

So if you run into anything in your area that you think we should know about, write it up and send it along to NCHEC Alert, 7373 147th Street, Apple Valley, MN 55124.

It could be the story of how a reverse mortgage improved someone's life. Or it could be a new product or a lending practice that you find questionable. Either way, if it's important enough for you to send, it's important enough for us to know about.

Spreading the Word

Just talking about what you've learned in this book may alert others to the new possibilities that reverse mortgages present.

Who knows? A casual comment here or there might be the link between your new knowledge and someone else's need. And if that need can be met with a reverse mortgage, then you will have done more than educate yourself.

Even if you conclude that reverse mortgages don't fit your situation now - or ever - your knowledge of this topic might lead others in different circumstances to reverse mortgage solutions that work for them.

So don't put a bushel barrel over what you've learned. Spread the word. Home equity is now a true retirement nest egg. And at some point, that might make a big difference in your life or someone else's.

It might even be the answer to someone's prayers.

Acknowledgements

In a previous book three years ago, I acknowledged 60 individuals who had contributed to the development of reverse mortgages. Now I'd like to highlight some groups who have made especially important contributions since then.

HUD-certified counselors have been essential to the success of the single largest reverse mortgage program. Working for nonprofit and public agencies, they have helped thousands of consumers identify and evaluate their options. Many have gone beyond the call of duty to forge difficult solutions when none initially appeared possible.

A variety of government officials have developed ground-breaking elements of federal policy on reverse mortgages. The effort has required inordinate doses of creativity and innovation, and the results have given needed direction to market development.

Particularly important has been the work of the Securities and Exchange Commission, the Federal Reserve Board, the Department of Housing and Urban Development, the Federal Trade Commission, and Senate and House Banking Committees.

Private product developers have continued bringing forth and refining new ideas. To their credit, their generic contributions to overall market development have in some cases actually exceeded even their own enlightened self-interest.

Acknowledgements

The HECM program has worked because of the joint efforts of HUD staff, dedicated originators, the pioneering servicing of Wendover Funding, and the staunch support of Fannie Mae. Basic systems development may not be glamorous. But I ask you, where would we be without it?

The single most important group by far has been all the consumers who have investigated these programs. Their views have been the foremost influence on market development. (So be sure to share your knowledge and opinions. Continuing progress toward a mature reverse mortgage market depends on it.)

In three short years we've gone from a list of 60 contributors to literally hundreds of them. But thank goodness two in particular have remained the same: Bronwyn Belling and Donald Redfoot of the AARP.

Bronwyn's major role has been the care and feeding of the HECM counseling network. Don's has been the creation of federal policy.

It's been my good fortune to have worked more closely with both of them than either might want to admit. So I know how central their skill and dedication have been to the sound growth of this idea. They have also taught me there's absolutely no substitute for good company in the vineyard.

Ken Scholen
Apple Valley, Minnesota   Thanksgiving Day, 1994

Appendix A
Total Loan Cost (TLC)
Rate Calculations

TLC rates begin with the projected total amount owed at the end of a reverse mortgage - as limited by non-recourse or equity conservation features. The TLC rate is the annual average percent that generates this "future value" when taken against all the cash advances (including annuity advances) the borrower receives for purposes other than financing loan costs (including annuity purchases, insurance premiums, origination fees, closing and servicing costs, and all other costs).

Here are sample keystrokes (on an HP 12C calculator) for figuring the TLC on a loan that provides monthly advances of $350 for 12 years and generates a total debt of $115,000.

- ☐ f CLEAR FIN 12 g 12X (144)
- ☐ 350 CHS PMT (-350)
- ☐ 115,000 FV (115,000)
- ☐ g BEG i (1.0219661)
- ☐ g 12X = 12.263593

The recent federal law requiring TLC disclosure was based on this algorithm developed by the National Center for Home Equity Conversion in 1989 (in the first edition of its "Financial Guide to Reverse Mortgages") and adopted by the U. S. Department of Housing and Urban Development in 1990 (for its "HECM" plan).

When the Fed finalizes its regulations to implement the new TLC disclosure, some details of its calculations may differ slightly from the methods used by NCHEC and HUD. For example, the Fed may use initial rather than expected rates in calculating the total amount owed. This would not alter the basic patterns and comparisons in this book. Once the regulations become effective, they will define the official standard for determining TLC rates.

311

Appendix B
Reverse Mortgage Lenders
November, 1994

The HUD/HECM Plan (Chapter 11)

AL -   Home Mortgagee; 800-669-8226
Homestead Mortgage; 404-324-2274
Reverse Mortgage Co; 800-588-8044
Senior Income; 800-774-6266
United Savings Bank; 205-237-6668

AR -   Home Mortgagee; 800-669-8226
Reverse Mortgage Co; 800-336-3135
Senior Income; 800-774-6266

AZ -   Directors Mortgage; 800-442-4966 X2201
Farwest Mortgage; 602-661-5545
First Mortgage; 800-456-0569
Rio Salado Mortgage; 602-345-8800
Sun American; 602-832-4343
Unity Mortgage; 800-334-9057

CA -   ARCS Mortgage; 800-237-2727
Directors Mortgage; 800-442-4966 X2201
Farwest Mortgage; 800-310-5568
Mical Mortgage; 619-452-8522
Unity Mortgage; 800-334-9057
Village Home Loans; 408-274-3081
Western Residential; 916-381-2000

CO -   Amerifirst Mortgage; 800-473-6467
Directors Mortgage; 800-442-4966 X2201
Home Mortgagee; 800-669-8226
Unity Mortgage; 800-358-8012
Wendover Funding; 800-843-0480

CT -   Amerifirst Mortgage; 800-473-6467
Constitution Mortgage; 203-237-0007
Hartford Funding; 516-588-9300, 718-470-6410
Home Mortgagee; 800-669-8226

312

HUD/HECM, continued

DE - Amerifirst Mortgage; 800-473-6467
Home Mortgagee; 800-669-8226
International Mortgage; 800-581-7806
Unity Mortgage; 800-368-3254

DC - Amerifirst Mortgage; 800-473-6467
International Mortgage; 800-581-7806
Unity Mortgage; 800-368-3254

FL - Brasota Mortgage; 813-746-6119
Builders Financial; 305-476-8181
Directors Mortgage; 800-442-4966 X2201
Homeowners & Investors; 407-533-6070
Bank of America; 800-772-6772
Navy Orlando Credit; 407-644-1100
Pinnacle Financial; 800-421-5626
Pointe Savings; 407-395-3155
Unity Mortgage; 800-588-8044

GA - Allatoona Savings; 404-952-0606
Home Mortgagee; 800-669-8226
Homestead Mortgage; 800-941-2274
Sunshine Mortgage; 800-966-0255
Tucker Federal; 404-938-1222
Unity Mortgage; 800-588-8044

HI - ARCS Mortgage; 808-263-6602
Directors Mortgage; 800-442-4966 X2201
First Hawaiian; 800-421-6284

ID - Directors Mortgage; 800-442-4966 X2201
Home Mortgagee; 800-669-8226
Investors West; 800-281-3338
Unity Mortgage; 800-334-9057

IL - Dependable Mortgage; 708-862-5969
Directors Mortgage; 708-495-6800
First Suburban; 708-934-1111
NBD Bank; 708-518-7100
Senior Income; 800-774-6266,
Unity Mortgage; 800-880-7740
WestAmerica; 708-916-9299

HUD/HECM, continued

IN - Dependable Mortgage; 708-862-5969
Home Mortgagee; 800-669-8226
Reverse Mortgage Co; 800-860-6983
Senior Income; 800-774-6266

IA - Allied Mortgage; 515-224-7100
Senior Income; 800-774-6266
Unity Mortgage; 800-880-7740

KS - Directors Mortgage; 800-442-4966 X2201
Home Mortgagee; 800-669-8226
James B Nutter; 816-531-2345
Senior Income; 800-774-6266
Unity Mortgage; 800-336-3135

KY - Home Mortgagee; 800-669-8226
Senior Income; 800-774-6266
Tri-County Mortgage; 606-523-1076
Unity Mortgage; 800-860-6983

LA - Home Mortgagee; 504-830-4747
Mortgage Co-op; 504-455-4000
Unity Mortgage; 800-336-3135

MA - Amerifirst Mortgage; 800-473-6467
Directors Mortgage; 800-378-5060

ME - Maine State Housing; 207-626-4600
Unity Mortgage; 800-832-5251

MD - Amerifirst Mortgage; 800-473-6467
Carroll Co Bank; 301-848-8100
Home Mortgagee; 800-669-8226
Home Equity Conversions; 800-310-4322
Hart Mortgage; 800-753-7878
International Mortgage; 800-581-7806
Unity Mortgage; 800-368-3254

MI - Bay Creek Mortgage; 800-968-5151
North Bank; 517-685-3519
Home Mortgagee; 800-669-8226
Senior Income; 800-774-6266
Unity Mortgage; 800-433-8485

HUD/HECM, continued

MN -   Heigl Mortgage; 612-831-6644
Home Mortgagee; 800-669-8226
Meridian Bank; 612-298-1402
Richfield Bank; 612-861-8339
Unity Mortgage; 800-880-7740

MO -   Amerifirst Mortgage; 800-473-6467
Directors Mtge; 800-442-4966 X2201
Home Mortgagee; 800-669-8226
James B Nutter; 816-531-2345
Senior Income; 800-774-6266
Unity Mortgage; 800-336-3135

MS -   Amerifirst Mortgage; 800-473-6467
Unity Mortgage; 800-533-7771

MT -   Amerifirst Mortgage; 800-473-6467
Intermountain Mortgage; 406-652-3000
Unity Mortgage; 800-334-9057

NE -   Commercial Federal; 402-554-9200
Unity Mortgage; 800-358-8012

NV -   ARCS Mortgage; 702-877-0556
Directors Mortgage; 800-442-4966 X2201; 702-454-2870
Unity Mortgage; 800-334-9057
WestAmerica Mortgage; 702-796-7990

NH -   CFX Bank; 603-352-2502
Directors Mortgage; 800-442-4966 X2201
First Deposit; 603-286-4348 X11
Home Mortgagee; 800-669-8226
Unity Mortgage; 800-832-5251

NJ -   Amerifirst Mortgage; 800-473-6467
Hart Mortgage; 800-753-7878
Interchange State Bank; 201-703-2265
Pioneer Mortgage; 800-222-0057
Unity Mortgage; 800-487-0088

NM -   Directors Mortgage; 800-442-4966 X2201
Home Mortgagee; 800-669-8226
Unity Mortgage; 800-358-8012

HUD/HECM, continued

NY -   Amerifirst Mortgage; 800-473-6467
        ARCS Mortgage; (914)-473-4911
        Country Bank; 914-225-2265 X110
        Hartford Funding; 516-588-9300, 718-470-6410
        Home Mortgagee; 800-669-8226
        OnBank; 315-424-4011
        Rockwell Equities; 516-334-7900
        Saxon National Mortgage Bank; 800-660-1853
        Senior Income; 800-774-6266
        Unity Mortgage; 800-487-0088

NC -   Centura Bank; 800-879-5864
        First State; 910-227-8861
        Home Mortgagee; 800-669-8226
        Security Capital; 704-335-4400
        Unity Mortgage; 800-588-8044
        Wendover Funding; 800-568-9109

ND -   Directors Mortgage; 800-442-4966 X2201

OH -   Directors Mortgage; 800-442-4966 X2201
        Home Mortgagee; 800-669-8226
        Senior Income; 800-774-6266
        Unity Mortgage; 800-860-6983

OK -   Amerifirst Mortgage; 800-473-6467
        Senior Income; 800-774-6266
        Unity Mortgage; 800-336-3135

OR -   ARCS Mortgage; 800-640-4773
        Directors Mortgage; 800-442-4966 X2201
        Home Mortgagee; 800-669-8226
        Unity Mortgage; 800-334-9057

PA -   Amerifirst Mortgage; 800-473-6467
        Boulevard Mortgage; 215-633-8080
        Directors Mortgage; 800-442-4966 X2201
        Hart Mortgage; 800-753-7878
        Home Mortgagee; 800-669-8226
        International Mortgage; 800-581-7806
        PA Housing Finance Agency; 800-822-1174
        Phoenix Mortgage; 215-659-0800
        Pioneer Mortgage; 609-546-1700
        Reverse Mortgage Co; 800-487-0088

HUD/HECM, continued

RI -   Rhode Island Housing; 401-751-5566

SC -   Amerifirst Mortgage; 800-473-6467
               American Federal; 803-255-7444
               First Citizens Mortgage; 803-733-1449
               First Federal; 803-582-2391
               Home Mortgagee; 800-669-8226
               Unity Mortgage; 800-588-8044

TN -   Amerifirst Mortgage; 800-473-6467
               Home Mortgagee; 800-669-8226
               Senior Income; 800-774-6266
               Unity Mortgage; 800-588-8044

UT -   Amerifirst Mortgage; 800-473-6467
               Affiliated Mortgage; 801-255-1118
               AIM Mortgage; 801-485-9355
               Directors Mortgage; 800-442-4966 X2201
               Unity Mortgage; 800-358-8012

VT -   Amerifirst Mortgage; 800-473-6467
               Chittenden Bank; 802-660-2123
               Unity Mortgage; 800-832-5251

VA -   Ameribanc Savings; 703-658-5500
               Ampthill Financial; 804-743-3590
               Crestar Mortgage; 804-498-8702
               Directors Mortgage; 800-442-4966 X2201
               Home Mortgage Center; 703-671-1414
               International Mortgage; 703-981-1011
               Mortgage Capital; 703-941-0711
               Unity Mortgage; 800-368-3254

WA -   ARCS Mortgage; (206)-462-7055, -744-2727
               Directors Mortgage; 800-442-4966 X2201; 206-778-3402
               Home Mortgagee; 800-669-8226
               Investors Mortgage; 208-345-8153
               Senior Income; 800-774-6266
               Western States Mortgage; 800-828-2814
               Unity Mortgage; 800-334-9057

WV -   Home Mortgagee; 800-669-8226
               International Mortgage; 800-581-7806
               Senior Income; 800-774-6266
               Unity Mortgage; 800-368-3254

HUD/HECM, continued

WI - Directors Mortgage; 800-442-4966 X2201
First Financial; 414-547-9100
Heigl Mortgage; 612-831-6644
Home Mortgagee; 800-669-8226
Senior Income; 800-774-6266
Unity Mortgage; 800-880-7740

WY - Home Mortgagee; 800-669-8226
Unity Mortgage; 800-358-8012

The Household Plan (Chapter 12)

Available in Florida, Georgia, Illinois, Ohio,
Maryland, Michigan, and Virginia. Expected to
become available in California and other major
states during 1995.

Call 1-800-414-3837.

The HomeFirst Plan (Chapter 13)

Available in California, New Jersey, New York,
and Pennsylvania. Expected to become available
in other states during 1995.

Call 1-800-538-5569.

The Freedom Plan (Chapter 14)

Available in California only. Expected to become
available in other states during 1995.

Call 1-800-637-3336.

The Fannie Mae Plan (Chapter 15)

Expected to become available during 1995 through HUD/HECM lenders.

The Republic Plan (Chapter 16)

Expected to become available during 1995 through HUD/HECM lenders.

Fixed-Term Plans (Chapter 17)

AZ - Reverse Mortgage Program
602-997-6105; 602-623-0344

CA - Human Investment (San Mateo County)
415-348-6660
Independent Living (San Francisco)
415-863-1290
Life Services (Southern California)
818-547-0585

MA - HOME Program
617-451-0680

ME - Gardiner Savings
207-882-7571

MN - Senior Housing
612-645-0261

NY - Residential Housing Opportunities (Westchester)
914-428-0953

Public Sector Plans (Chapter 18)

See **Chapter 18** for locating *property tax deferral* programs and *deferred payment loans* for home repairs and improvements.

"Split-term" reverse mortgages are offered through state housing finance agencies in

Connecticut: 800-443-9946

Montana: 406-444-3040

New Hampshire: 800-640-7239

Appendix C
HUD/HECM Calculations

In the HUD/HECM program, there are three basic steps in calculating your cash advances:

1) use your age, home value, and interest rate to determine your "principal limit," which is the most cash you could possibly get at closing;

2) subtract from your principal limit any funds you need to use or set aside at closing, for example, to finance start-up costs or pay for repairs; and

3) use your "net" principal limit to figure out how much money you could get from any single type of loan advance, or any combination of types.

You begin by looking up your "principal limit factor" in a table published by HUD, and reproduced in this appendix. You need two pieces of information to do this: your age, and the expected interest rate on the loan.

If you are married or if more than one person owns your home, you must use the age of the youngest borrower.

You get the "expected annual average interest rate" from your lender. If the lender is charging interest at a fixed rate, then that is the rate you use. If the lender is charging an adjustable rate, then the "expected" rate is determined by a HUD formula the lender must use.

The "expected annual average interest rate" is the U. S. Treasury Securities rate adjusted to a constant maturity of ten years PLUS the "lender's margin." The lender's margin is the initial rate on the loan MINUS the one-year Treasury rate.

The purpose of this formula is to determine the financial market's best estimate of the average annual rate over the approximate term of HUD-HECM loans. You can find the Treasury rates every Tuesday in the "Money & Investing" section of The Wall Street Journal in a small box called "Key Interest Rates."

HUD/HECM Principal Limit Factor Table

Age	8%	9%	10%	11%	12%	13%	14%
62	0.37	0.3	0.25	0.2	0.17	0.14	0.12
63	0.38	0.31	0.26	0.21	0.18	0.15	0.13
64	0.39	0.32	0.27	0.22	0.19	0.16	0.14
65	0.41	0.34	0.28	0.23	0.2	0.17	0.14
66	0.42	0.35	0.29	0.25	0.21	0.18	0.15
67	0.43	0.36	0.3	0.26	0.22	0.19	0.16
68	0.44	0.37	0.32	0.27	0.23	0.2	0.17
69	0.45	0.39	0.33	0.28	0.24	0.21	0.18
70	0.47	0.4	0.34	0.29	0.25	0.22	0.19
71	0.48	0.41	0.36	0.31	0.27	0.23	0.2
72	0.49	0.43	0.37	0.32	0.28	0.25	0.22
73	0.51	0.44	0.39	0.34	0.29	0.26	0.23
74	0.52	0.46	0.4	0.35	0.31	0.27	0.24
75	0.54	0.47	0.42	0.37	0.32	0.29	0.26
76	0.55	0.49	0.43	0.38	0.34	0.3	0.27
77	0.57	0.5	0.45	0.4	0.36	0.32	0.29
78	0.58	0.52	0.47	0.42	0.37	0.34	0.3

Age	8%	9%	10%	11%	12%	13%	14%
79	0.6	0.54	0.48	0.43	0.39	0.35	0.32
80	0.61	0.55	0.5	0.45	0.41	0.37	0.34
81	0.63	0.57	0.52	0.47	0.43	0.39	0.35
82	0.64	0.59	0.54	0.49	0.45	0.41	0.37
83	0.66	0.6	0.55	0.51	0.47	0.43	0.39
84	0.67	0.62	0.57	0.53	0.48	0.45	0.41
85	0.69	0.64	0.59	0.55	0.5	0.47	0.43
86	0.7	0.65	0.61	0.56	0.52	0.49	0.45
87	0.72	0.67	0.62	0.58	0.54	0.51	0.47
88	0.73	0.69	0.64	0.6	0.56	0.53	0.49
89	0.74	0.7	0.66	0.62	0.58	0.55	0.52
90	0.76	0.72	0.68	0.64	0.61	0.57	0.54
95	0.83	0.81	0.78	0.75	0.73	0.7	0.68

After you find your principal limit factor, you have to find your "maximum claim amount." This figure is the lesser of

☐ the appraised value of your home *OR*

☐ HUD's "203-b-2" limit for your area.

Check with your nearest HUD lender (see **Appendix B**) to find the current 203-b-2 limit in your area.

Now that you know your principal limit factor and your maximum claim amount, you can figure out your principal limit. You do it by multiplication. For example, if your age is 75 and your interest rate is 10%, then your principal limit factor is .416. If your home is worth $100,000 and your 203-b-2 limit is greater, then your maximum claim amount is $100,000.

To get your principal limit, you just multiply .416 times $100,000. The result ($41,600) is the largest possible lump sum of cash you could get from the loan at closing provided you pay all start-up costs out of your own pocket. Your principal limit is the "present value" of the loan advances available to you.

If you're like most people, however, you wouldn't take all the money you could get in a single lump sum at closing. But you probably would want to use some of your principal limit to finance your start-up costs, for example.

If we assume those costs are about 4% of your home's value ($4,000), then your "net" principal limit would be $37,600. That's the largest amount you could get in a single lump sum at closing if you finance your start-up costs.

The net principal limit is also the number you use to generate all the other types of loan advances. You simply use the "time-value-of-money" formula built into most financial calculators.

For example, assume you want to put the full amount of your $37,600 net principal limit into a five-year term of monthly advances. You enter five years as the "N" or "term," $37,600 as the "present value," and 10.5% as the interest rate.

(You add 0.5% to the expected interest rate because the HUD insurance premium is charged in two parts: 2% at closing, plus 0.5% added to the periodic interest rate.) You also set the calculator for "beginning of the term" because the monthly loan advances begin at closing. The answer in this example is $801 per month for a five-year term.

To calculate monthly advances for a tenure plan, HUD uses a "term" equal to 100 minus your age. For more details on calculating loan advances, see HUD Handbook 4235.1.

- Adapted from **Retirement Income On The House**

Glossary

adjustable rate - an interest rate that changes based on changes in a published market rate

annuity - a monthly cash advance for life

appreciation - an increase in the value of a home

appraisal - an estimate of a home's market value

capital gains tax - a tax on increases in home value

closing - a meeting at which legal documents are signed to "close the deal" on a mortgage; the time at which a mortgage begins

creditline - a credit account that permits a borrower to control the timing and amount of the loan advances; also known as a "line-of-credit"

default - the failure of a borrower or lender to fulfill agreed-upon mortgage terms

deferred payment loans - reverse mortgages providing lump sums for repairing or improving homes

depreciation - a decrease in the value of a home

equity conservation - a feature permitting borrowers to pre-select their debt limit

fixed-term - a reverse mortgage that becomes due and payable on a specific date *home equity* - the value of a home minus any debt against it

home equity conversion - turning home equity into cash without having to leave your home or make regular loan repayments

joint tenancy - equal ownership rights held by two or more persons that survive the death of any owner

lifetime advances - fixed monthly loan advances for the rest of a borrower's life

leftover equity - net sale proceeds minus total amount owed

loan advances - payments made to a borrower, or to another party on behalf of a borrower

loan balance - the amount owed, including principal and interest; limited in a reverse mortgage by a non-recourse feature

loan term - the period of time from closing until the loan is due and payable

lump sum - a single loan advance of a substantial amount

maturity - when a loan becomes due and payable

mortgage - a legal document making a home available to a lender to satisfy a debt

non-recourse mortgage - a loan in which a lender may only look to the value of the home for repayment *origination* - the administrative process of setting up a mortgage, including the preparation of documents

percent of value pricing - a loan cost equaling a percent of a home's value at loan maturity

principal - see *loan advances*

property tax deferrals - reverse mortgages providing annual loan advances for paying property taxes

reverse annuity mortgage - a reverse mortgage in which a lump sum is used to purchase an annuity

reverse mortgage - a loan against home equity providing cash advances to a borrower and requiring no repayment until a future time

servicing - performing administrative functions on a loan after closing

shared appreciation - a loan cost related to any increase in the value of a home

tenure advances - fixed monthly loan advances for as long as a borrower lives in a home

term advances - fixed monthly loan advances for a specific period of time

Total Loan Cost (TLC) rate - the projected annual average cost of a reverse mortgage including all costs as limited by the non-recourse feature

Resources

American Association of Retired Persons (AARP). **Model State Law on Reverse Mortgages**, Washington, DC, 1990

American Bar Association. **Attorney's Guide to Home Equity Conversion**, Commission on Legal Problems of the Elderly, Washington, DC, 1992

Mayer, Christopher and Katerina Simons. "A New Look at Reverse Mortgages: Potential Market and Institutional Constraints," **New England Economic Review**, March/April, 1994

Phillips, William and Stephen Gwin. "Reverse Mortgages," **Transactions** (Vol. XLIV), Society of Actuaries, Schaumburg, IL, 1993

Scholen, Ken. **Retirement Income On The House; Cashing In On Your Home With A "Reverse" Mortgage**, National Center for Home Equity Conversion, Apple Valley, MN, 1994

Syzmanoski, Jr., Edward J. **The FHA Home Equity Conversion Mortgage Insurance Demonstration: A Model to Calculate Borrower Payments and Insurance Risk**, U. S. Department of Housing and Urban Development, Washington, DC, 1990

U. S. Department of Housing and Urban Development. **Evaluation of the Home Equity Conversion Mortgage Insurance Demonstration**, Washington, DC, 1994

U.S. Department of Housing and Urban Development, **Home Equity Conversion Mortgages; Hand book 4235.1 REV-1**, Washington DC, 1994

Index

About the Author

Ken Scholen founded and directs the National Center for Home Equity Conversion. Since 1978, he has promoted the development of reverse mortgages through research, training, consulting, publishing, and public policy analysis and advocacy. He edited the first book, organized the first national conferences, and conducted the first public research projects in the field.

Scholen has testified before four committees of Congress, and has keynoted conferences and led training sessions in 43 states. He has consulted with most of the reverse mortgage development efforts in the United States, and some in England, Canada, Spain, Australia, and Japan.

He helped establish and for ten years has provided consulting services to AARP's Home Equity Information Center. He has authored consumer guides for AARP, HUD, and NCHEC. More than 400,000 copies of his publications are currently in print.

Scholen originally proposed a federal program to insure reverse mortgages, assisted in drafting the initial HUD/HECM legislation, authored key technical amendments, led the effort to gain Congressional approval, consulted with HUD in designing the program, and has trained 3,000 HUD consumer counselors, private lenders, and HUD staff members.

He developed the "total loan cost" method of analyzing reverse mortgages adopted by the U. S. Department of Housing and Urban Development and the Federal Reserve Board. He also advocated the specialized reverse mortgage accounting methodology adopted by the U. S. Securities and Exchange Commission.

In other areas, Scholen has directed a state board on aging, co-founded a statewide senior advocacy coalition, developed an innovative senior housing facility, directed a comprehensive senior services organization, conducted research in city government, and lobbied for six years on child welfare issues. He was a founding board member of United Seniors Health Cooperative (DC) and the Wisconsin Partnership for Housing Development.

About NCHEC

The National Center for Home Equity Conversion is an independent, not-for-profit organization devoted to the development of sound home equity conversion opportunities for homeowners.

NCHEC conducts educational seminars for consumers, counselors, and consumer organizations. It provides research and consultation services for product and program developers, public policymakers, and the media. The Center collects and publishes a variety of materials, serving as a national clearinghouse on reverse mortgages and other home equity conversion plans.

NCHEC received initial start-up funding from the Florence V. Burden Foundation, the Retirement Research Foundation, the Levi Strauss Foundation, and the Kimberly Clark Foundation. Ongoing support comes primarily from federal and state research and training grants, consulting for consumer organizations, and sales of publications.

Established in 1981 in Madison, Wisconsin, the Center grew out of state and federal research projects on home equity conversion. NCHEC moved to Minnesota in 1989, and is now located at 7373 147th Street West, Apple Valley, MN 55124; telephone (612) 953-4474.

NCHEC Services

The National Center for Home Equity Conversion supplies speakers on reverse mortgages for conventions, conferences, seminars, and training sessions.

The Center also provides consulting services and develops seminars and training sessions on reverse mortgages to fit specialized needs.

NCHEC Publications

Retirement Income On The House; Cashing In On Your Home With A "Reverse" Mortgage by Ken Scholen (1992, revised 1994), with a preface by Jane Bryant Quinn. An elementary introduction to the basic consumer economics of reverse mortgages. Features simple, step-by-step explanations of key analytic concepts and examples of typical consumers. Discusses alternatives to reverse mortgages. Named *Best Book on Financial Services for the Elderly* by the National Association of Area Agencies on Aging. 340 pages, 32 tables.

Marketing Reverse Mortgages by Ken Scholen (1995). Includes a capsule history of reverse mortgages in the United States, an analysis of barriers to consumer response, and marketing recommendations for a multi-product environment. 44 pages.

Sale Leaseback Guide & Model Documents by Trudy Ernst and Maurice Weinrobe (1984). Discusses important legal and financial issues that parties to a sale leaseback should consider. Provides guidance to sellers, buyers, and attorneys. Financial analysis covers the sales price, seller financing, the lease, and financial risks. Legal analysis explains sale leaseback agreement, secured promissory note, deed of trust, lease, and memorandum of lease. 84 pages.

8/8/95

Order Blank

Please send the following NCHEC publications:

☐ **Retirement Income On The House** ($19.00)

☐ **Marketing Reverse Mortgages** ($29.00)

☐ **Sale Leaseback Guide** ($39.00)

Enclosed is $_____ payable to "NCHEC".

Send the publications to:

NAME_____

ADDRESS_____

_____

_____ZIP_____

- -

Send order blank and payment to:

> **NCHEC - Suite 115**
> **7373 - 147 St W**
> **Apple Valley, MN 55124**

336